"According to the Census Bureau, more than one in four children live without a father in the home, and most of the societal ills in America can be traced back to fatherlessness. Additionally, few of the men who are in the home are engaged. There is no greater need in our culture than for men to recover their identity and take their place of leadership as strong and courageous men in their families, communities, and our culture. LTG Jerry Boykin and Dr. Kenyn Cureton offer a timely book that makes the case for biblical masculinity from the book of Joshua. It provides real solutions to the problems we face."

— *Honorable Ken Blackwell*, former U.S. Ambassador to the UN Human Rights Commission, former mayor of Cincinnati

"It's not easy being a real man today! Our gender-confused culture considers masculinity to be 'toxic.' But God's Word paints a different picture of manhood straight from the hand of our Creator. *Strong and Courageous*, drawing from the life of Joshua, offers key biblical insights into real manhood as God intended.

"Joshua—a key member of Israel's first twelve-man recon team, and ultimately the commanding general of the nation's entire army—is a solid example of that godly manhood. It is not surprising then that Joshua happens to be the favorite Bible character of my dear friend, LTG (RET.) Jerry Boykin! Most guys have seen *Blackhawk Down*, where Boykin commanded our elite Special Ops warriors in that tough and tense operation. In his thirty-six years in the Army, Boykin was often acting as America's point man—intimately involved in virtually every major U.S. military action you've ever heard of (and many you've never heard of because of their covert nature). Jerry's lifetime of faithfulness to Jesus has made him a most effective mentor to me and many, many others.

"In his new book, *Strong and Courageous*, Jerry picks up where *Man to Man* left off—demonstrating here how the five key elements of manhood play out in the life of Joshua, the powerful warrior and spiritual leader of an entire nation. We need such men today! I strongly suggest you buy a few copies, give them to your battle buddies, and meet weekly around its principles. It will make you all better men . . . something our nation so desperately needs in these troubled days. Step up, strong and courageous, to biblical manhood."

    — *Dr. Stu Weber*, pastor and author

"Joshua has been a favorite in my Bible study group over the many years we've been meeting. The prime reason being he is a quintessential example of how a man should follow God no matter the cost, with faith and selflessness. General Boykin and Dr. Cureton have delivered a book for men at a critical time in our country and history. Every man will be strengthened and given clear vision for leading their families and communities by reading *Strong and Courageous*. Better yet, buy enough to facilitate a men's Bible study group!"

    — *LtCol Oliver L. North* USMC (Ret), bestselling author of *Tragic Consequences*, founder of Fidelis Publishing and Fidelis Media

STRONG
AND **COURAGEOUS**

A Call to Biblical Manhood

LTG (RET.) JERRY BOYKIN
and DR. KENYN M. CURETON

FIDELIS
PUBLISHING

FIDELIS PUBLISHING
ISBN: 9781736620687
ISBN (eBook): 9781736620694

Strong and Courageous: A Call to Biblical Manhood
© 2022 Family Research Council

Cover design by Diana Lawrence • Interior layout by Lisa Parnell • Edited by Amanda Varian

Discounted books at www.faithfultext.com. For information about special discounts for bulk purchases, please contact BulkBooks.com, call 1-888-959-5153 or email - cs@bulkbooks.com

FIDELIS
PUBLISHING

Fidelis Publishing, LLC (Sterling, VA • Nashville, TN)
fidelispublishing.com

Published in cooperation with
Family Research Council – www.frc.org

Manufactured in the United States of America

10 9 8 7 6 5 4 3 2 1

Contents

Foreword vii

Introduction 1

1. **Men Needed** 7
   Man's Problem
   God's Solution
   Stand Courageous

2. **Man as a Provider** 33
   Devotion to Direction – Joshua 1:1–9
   Worth of Work – Joshua 1:10–18
   Importance of Identity – Joshua 5:1–12

3. **Man as an Instructor** 65
   Times to Teach – Joshua 4:1–24
   Learn to Discern – Joshua 2; 7; 9
   Rehearse Your History – Joshua 24:1–13

4. **Man as a Defender** 103
   Fight for Your Family – Joshua 6; 8
   Defend against Defeat – Joshua 7:1–26
   Protect the Powerless – Joshua 10:1–11

5. **Man as a Battle Buddy** 133
   Friendship Forged in the Fire – Joshua 14:6–15
   Iron Sharpens Iron – Joshua 7:16–20; 9:22–27; 22:10–34
   Mentor Other Men – Exodus 17; 24; 32–33; Numbers 27;
      Deuteronomy 31

6. **Man as a Chaplain** 171
   Face to Face – Joshua 5:13–15

Daily Devotion – Joshua 8:30–35
Call to Commitment – Joshua 24:14–30

Conclusion 211

Book Study Discipleship Tool 213

Stand Courageous Pledge 217

Stand on the Word Bible Reading Plan 219

About the Authors 221

Notes 223

Foreword

One of the greatest needs in America today is for men to follow the biblical admonition originally given to Joshua to be strong and courageous—to be courageous in obeying God and serving Him! Certainly, the author of this book, Family Research Council executive vice president, LTG (RET.) Jerry Boykin, models that call.

General Boykin served his country for over thirty-six years in the United States Army. From 1978–1993 he was assigned in various capacities to Delta Force. Not only was he a founding member of the Delta Force, he has also led Green Berets and other Special Operations units into battle on numerous occasions. Among his many successful operations was "Operation Urgent Fury" in Marxist-held Grenada in 1983, where he was shot in the arm with a .50-caliber round. Doctors wanted to remove his limb, but by the grace of God, he has full use of it today. Also notable was "Operation Just Cause" in Panama, where he led Delta Force operators to free American journalist Kurt Muse and depose dictator Manuel Noriega. Perhaps his most famous command was during the Battle of Mogadishu in Somalia in 1993, which was made into a major movie titled *Black Hawk Down*. Vastly outnumbered and outgunned, his Delta Force operators and Rangers prevailed. It goes without saying, General Boykin's citations for valor are too numerous to list. The general truly is a man's man.

Though he retired from active military service, the general continues to serve this country. When he took the oath, swearing to "support and defend the Constitution of the United States against all enemies, foreign and domestic" with the help of God, he meant it and he's still doing it. Not only is General Boykin a decorated military hero, he is an ordained minister, and a popular author. Consequently, his courage and leadership extend far beyond the physical battlefield into the spiritual war raging for the soul of America. It is not surprising men and masculinity have become the preferred target of the enemy in America. Without courageous men who will stand and defend what is true and right, there is little hope for our nation. That is why I am grateful General Boykin and Family Research Council have launched a new ministry to men called Stand Courageous. I'm grateful for his leadership and I am honored to provide this foreword and pleased to recommend his book, *Strong and Courageous: A Call to Biblical Manhood*.

In the Scriptures, there are few better models for men than Joshua, God's general. That biblical book and character is the special focus of this book. *Strong and Courageous* gives modern men their marching orders. As a follow-up to General Boykin's excellent book *Man to Man*, this new book takes the five basic roles of provider, instructor, defender, battle buddy, and chaplain and seeks to illustrate each of them in the life of Joshua. General Boykin's book is filled with biblical and experiential wisdom to help outline the responsibilities of every God-honoring man. May this book, *Strong and Courageous*, aid you in becoming the loving husband, faithful father, and godly mentor God has called you to be in your family, church, and community.

> — Tony Perkins, Family Research Council's fourth
> and longest-serving president

Introduction

As Ed Byers and his fellow members of SEAL Team Six trudged through the bitter cold of eastern Afghanistan, they wondered what they would find when they reached their target—a compound full of Taliban fighters.[1]

It was mid-December, and Afghanistan's mountain-filled Laghman Province is one of the most rugged places in a country filled with rough terrain. It's close to the border of Pakistan and has been especially hard-hit by years of war, with nearly half of its villages destroyed. And it remains a stronghold of well-armed, aggressive Islamic radicals.

Senior Chief Petty Officer Byers is no ordinary sailor. With nine combat tours, two Purple Hearts, and five Bronze Stars, Byers was tested and proven time and again in the crucible of combat. For his actions on December 9, 2012, Ed Byers received another award, the nation's highest for military heroism—the Congressional Medal of Honor.

SEAL Team 6 was on its way to rescue captured American Dr. Dilip Joseph—medical director of Morning Star Development, a nonprofit that trains Afghans to build strong communities, including teaching medical personnel. Dr. Joseph had made ten trips to Afghanistan from 2008 through 2012, working with Afghan doctors, nurses, and other medical professionals,

1

equipping them to better serve the many needy people all around them.[2]

But everything changed on December 5, 2012. As he was returning to Kabul from a rural clinic with two Afghan associates, their car was stopped by four men—men with guns. They were Taliban.

So on December 8, Byers and his SEALs unit made a difficult night journey in freezing weather to the Taliban where Dr. Joseph was being held. Called a "no fail" mission, the SEALs knew that the stakes couldn't be higher—not only were their lives at grave risk, but so were those of Dr. Joseph and the other prisoners. There would be no negotiation.

After quietly creeping up to the compound where the Taliban were hiding Dr. Joseph, Byers and Petty Officer First Class Nicolas Checque burst in. Byers "stood in the doorway fully exposed to enemy fire," reports his 2016 Medal of Honor citation, "while ripping down six layers of heavy blankets fastened to the inside ceiling and walls to clear a path for the rescue force."[3] He then saw Checque fall mortally wounded, but advanced on a Taliban fighter who was aiming an AK-47 directly at him.

Byers took him down. By the time the bullets had stopped flying, he had killed another Taliban fighter and pinned a third to a wall until another SEAL got him. And he threw himself atop Dr. Joseph to protect him from any of the Islamists who might try to kill him. "His bold and decisive actions under fire saved the lives of the hostage and several of his teammates," says his citation.

There's much more to say about this remarkable warrior and patriot. Two things are worth noting. First is Ed's deep devotion to God. He is serious about his faith, leading prayer groups when he was in the Marine Corps and now serving as a member of the Knights of Columbus.[4] Second is one of his mentors, namely his dad, Edward C. Byers, Sr. He too served in the U.S. Navy during World War II and now rests in Arlington Cemetery. Like many men from the "Greatest Generation," he didn't talk about his military service, but the American flag was always flying outside their Ohio farm home, and the Fourth of July was the most celebrated holiday of the year.

At its heart, Ed Byers' story is grounded in a deep commitment to God and country and the things that have made it great. If America is to survive, let alone thrive, we need more men like Ed Byers—not necessarily men who can duplicate the extraordinary heroism Byers displayed on that frigid early morning in Afghanistan, but men who will nevertheless be strong and courageous in all walks and situations of life.

How to Use This Book

Strong and Courageous offers a battle plan for men—a call to biblical manhood—where we can be reminded of our God-given responsibility in a culture swiftly turning away from God's design. The book of Joshua and his leadership will be the focus of our study for the balance of this book as we consider the five major roles and responsibilities of men as leaders:

1. Provider
2. Instructor
3. Defender
4. Battle Buddy
5. Chaplain

This study is designed ideally for small groups of men—we call them Battle Buddy Groups—men who are ready to be real with each other and delve deeper into God's Word to learn what it is to be a man and to lead others.

Battle Buddy Group Guides

In addition to the *Strong and Courageous* book, Battle Buddy Group Guides are provided at the end of each chapter. These guides correspond to six weeks of focus on the book and are designed to be used in a smaller group of three or four men for deeper discussion, prayer, and accountability. Each week's guide includes a brief story written by General Boykin, as well as a "Group Debrief" for smaller-group discussion written by Kenyn Cureton. Here is some further explanation:

- *What Is a Battle Buddy Group?* A Battle Buddy Group is a closed group three or four men join by invitation and commitment. This is different than an open small group or a Bible study (meaning everyone is welcome). The smaller nature of the group allows a more concentrated level of accountability and opens discussions that are more personal than in a standard group meeting.
- *Why Join a Battle Buddy Group?* We're not meant to live the Christian life alone. We all need support as we seek to live a life pleasing to God. Connecting with a handful of guys who are likely going through or have been through some of the same struggles encourages participation from you and from those who may not feel comfortable opening up in a larger group. Battle Buddy Groups offer a great opportunity for personal growth and meaningful friendships with guys like you. Additionally, Battle Buddy Groups give other men permission to speak into your life for encouragement, accountability, and prayer.
- *What Will Be Required?* The goal of Battle Buddy Groups is deeper discipleship and accountability. That takes commitment. Plan to meet for one hour. Be willing to participate each week. Be willing to be open and honest about

your spiritual condition and about ways you're struggling. Be willing to hold what's said in this group in confidence. Confidentiality builds trust with one another. Be willing to pray and support one another. Finally, allow the relationships to extend beyond the Battle Buddy Group meeting.

Let's Get Started

Is it any wonder the family structure is faltering, even disintegrating, given the all-out assault on the American male? As a result, many men are confused and feel frustrated because of the overwhelmingly negative messages. What is a real man supposed to be? What are our God-given roles and responsibilities? Thankfully, the Bible offers transcendent truth to guide us, and we have a great example in the biblical character of Joshua. Let's get started!

CHAPTER 1

Men Needed

Masculinity in America has never been under such attack as it is today. We have now reached a place in contemporary culture where the term itself is considered offensive. The consistent message proliferated is that masculinity, by nature, is bad and even the root cause of many of the problems plaguing the nation. Everything from sexism to racism to pedophilia has been blamed on "Toxic Masculinity." Some colleges and universities are now offering classes on how to deprogram or otherwise be "delivered" from this threatening phenomenon called masculinity.

Man's Problem?

Tucker Carlson of Fox News did an eye-opening, four-part series on "Men in America," and his conclusion was that "men are failing in body, mind and spirit . . . when men fail all of us suffer."[1] Here are some of the major findings from Carlson's series, with additional data that bolsters an already compelling case:

Health Problems

- Physically, men are failing; half of young men failed the U.S. Army's entry-level fitness requirements. Fully 70% of American men are overweight or obese, compared to 59% of American women.

- American men seem to be becoming "less male." Sperm counts are down 60% since 1970. Average levels of testosterone have dropped by 1% every year at all age levels since 1987. So the average forty-year-old male in 2017 has 30% less testosterone than a forty-year-old male in 1987. Lower testosterone levels lead to depression, lethargy, weight gain, and lowered cognitive ability.
- Men live five years less than women. One of the reasons is addiction. Men are twice as likely to become alcoholics and twice as likely to die of a drug overdose. In New Hampshire, 73% of the opioid overdose deaths were men.
- Men account for 77% of all suicide deaths. There has been a 43% increase between 1997 and 2014. White males are disproportionately represented.

Behavior Problems

- Problems start when males are young. Relative to girls, boys are failing in school. Boys are involved in far more disciplinary cases than girls.
- One in five high school boys has been diagnosed with some sort of hyperactivity disorder compared with just one in eleven girls. Many of the boys were medicated for it, and the long-term effects are yet to be known but do appear to include depression later in life.
- Men account for over 90% of inmates in prison.
- The majority of ISIS recruits are fatherless boys.
- Men are the perpetrators in all the mass shootings, with a noticeably large percentage of them being young men. About 90% of mass shooters were brought up in homes with minimal or no involvement by their father.[2]

Pornography Problems[3]

Among males over thirteen years old, pornography is a pernicious and pervasive problem:

- Seven in ten use porn at least on occasion (69%). Half use it monthly or more often (51%). One in ten American males views porn daily (11%).
- Only three in ten say they never seek out porn (31%); two-thirds come across porn at least monthly (66%); one in five comes across porn daily, even if they're not seeking it (20%); one in ten never comes across it (10%).
- Less than half consider viewing pornography wrong (44%).
- Two-thirds of porn users are comfortable with how much they use (68%).
- Only one in twenty porn users says it sometimes hurts their relationships (5%).

Education Problems

- More girls than boys graduate from high school; considerably more women than men go to and graduate from college.
- Women are far more likely to go to graduate school and pursue doctoral degrees. They are the majority of students in law and medical schools.
- Women earn 62% of associate degrees, 57% of bachelor's degrees, 60% of master's degrees, and 52% of doctorates.
- Women are scoring higher on IQ tests than men.

Wage-Earning Problems

- Between 1979–2010, working age men with only high school degrees saw their real hourly wages drop by 20%. Over the same period, women with high school degrees saw their wages rise.

- Approximately 7 million men ages 25–54 do not have jobs. That is 10% of the prime-age male labor force in the U.S. That is the highest rate in the industrialized world.
- Far fewer young men get married than did a few decades ago, and fewer stay married. About one in five children live only with their mothers. That is double the rate of 1970.
- Young adult men are more likely to live with a parent than with a spouse or a partner.
- Single women buy their own homes at twice the rate of single men. More women have driver's licenses than men. There are more women managers than men in America.

Relationship Problems

- Children do best when there is not just a father, but a biological father. The biological father is less likely to drop out of the picture when there is marriage.
- However, 40% of children are born to an unmarried mother, and 40% of men who father children out of wedlock in a domestic partnership never see their children after two years.
- Boys with fathers do well, but boys without fathers do terribly on more than seventy different measures, including postponed gratification, depression, drinking, and drug addiction.
- When fathers are asked for and valued, they come back into the picture; when they are not, they drop out.
- The trend is that fewer families are forming, and more children are growing up without fathers at home.[4]

All these statistics are alarming. They clearly demonstrate that we have a crisis in America, and men are at the heart of it. This is nothing new. God's people also faced a crisis involving men as a result of their disobedience and God's impending judgment. The prophet Isaiah reports on this in chapter 3:1–15, where he announces that part of God's judgment is the removal of men who are leaders and what will happen in the vacuum.

Read Isaiah 3:1–15 and answer the following questions:

- In the prophecy of coming judgment, Isaiah identifies the group of men who will be removed in verses 1–3. Can you identify what lines up with the five biblical roles we are focusing on in this study (see the Contents page)?
- In verses 4–5 and 12, we read that in the vacuum of godly male leadership three groups will take over. What are these groups? Do any of those line up with the statistical data you read earlier?

"Toxic" Masculinity

If all these problems were not enough, masculinity is under assault in the culture. For a generation, the culture used terms like "macho" or "stud" to describe the kind of masculinity that men were expected to aspire to. Now that is discouraged, even condemned. The buzzword today is "toxic masculinity," which was once relegated to liberal progressive women's studies in university classrooms.[5] Have you seen the Gillette video that went viral?[6] It was a razor ad from 2019 that went straight at the issue of masculinity being "toxic." Look it up on the web if you have not seen it. You'll notice the spin on their longtime slogan, "The Best a Man Can Get." The ad proposes to reject the slogan and challenge male viewers to confront #MeToo sexual harassment and other issues of "toxic masculinity" that manifest in acts like bullying and catcalling and worse. No one disputes that sexual harassment and bullying are societal ills. The issue here is that Gillette's recent ad suggests that the traditional masculinity symbolized in their classic "The Best a Man Can Get" ad campaign was somehow part of the problem and should be abandoned. Gillette's updated definition of "misogyny" is skewed to fit the narrative of the radical left in America. As a result, Gillette has seen their profits and stock go down dramatically.

The Gillette ad came after the American Psychological Association (APA) released its first-ever guidelines last year for psychologists working with boys and men who are socialized to conform to what they term as "traditional masculinity ideology"—which it says can hinder them from exploring what it means to be male. So what does "toxic masculinity" or "traditional masculinity ideology" mean? APA researchers contend that "toxic masculinity" is the result of teaching boys they can't express emotion openly—that they have to be tough all the time or otherwise they are weak. According to the APA, these cultural lessons have been linked to "aggression and violence," leaving boys and men at "disproportionate risk for school discipline, academic challenges and health disparities," including cardiovascular problems and substance abuse. "Men are overrepresented in prisons, are more likely than women to commit violent crimes and are at greatest risk of being a victim of violent crime," the APA wrote.[7]

So as a result, there is an effort by liberal progressives to eradicate so-called "toxic masculinity." One Ivy League school is offering courses. The Brown University website says that society's definition of masculinity may be toxic to men's health, causing them to die at younger ages, adding that the way in which men have been socialized also "plays into the type of violence that exists in college communities."

"BWell is investing in creating safe spaces for men to unpack all of the things they have learned about masculinity and what it means to be a man," the website says. "The goal is to help those socialized as men to unlearn some of the notions that have led to such profound harm being enacted toward others and toward themselves."[8]

In other words, at today's universities, masculinity is almost never discussed except in negative terms, usually with the word "toxic" attached. When girls and women are discussed, the question is always about how to help them do better. When boys and men are mentioned, it's almost always assumed that males are some sort of a problem.[9] And it is spreading even to military training. West Point cadets are now exposed to a curriculum that denounces "toxic masculinity." One cadet commented: "I'm being taught how not to be a man."[10] Furthermore, this notion of "safe space" is one of the last things we need to be promulgating to anyone in the military, yet we have a generation of men as well as women who believe that such a phenomenon actually exists today.

Think for a moment of the morning of June 6, 1944, at a place called Normandy on the shores of Nazi-occupied France. One hundred and sixty thousand men crossed the beaches that morning under withering artillery and small arms fire directed at these young men in an effort to disrupt the American formations and turn back the invasion. Do you think these warriors were looking for a "safe space"? Well, actually they were—on the other side of the German lines after defeating them in battle and overrunning their positions. These American men knew their job was to kill, capture, and put to flight every German soldier on that beach, and only then would they find rest and a "safe space." This is a terribly damaging concept to be pushing on a generation of men and women who will be called to defend our nation against our enemies.

Now, there is no excuse for bad behavior by men, especially when it comes to sexual harassment, but the social engineers in our culture are taking us too far. What we are seeing is the de-masculinization of men, or maybe more specifically, the feminization of men, and that is ultimately harmful to marriages, families, churches, and American society as a whole.

As we read in Isaiah 3:4–7, we are seeing what happens to a culture when men are missing or fail to be what God intends:

> And I will make boys their princes, and infants shall rule over them. And the people will oppress one another, every one his fellow and every one his neighbor; the youth will be insolent to the elder, and the despised to the honorable. For a man will take hold of his brother in the house of his father, saying: "You have a cloak; you shall be our leader, and this ' heap of ruins shall be under your rule"; in that day he will speak out, saying: "I will not be a healer; in my house there is neither bread nor cloak; you shall not make me leader of the people."

We read of the desperation for a man to step up and lead in the midst of crisis, and the last verse lines up with what we are seeing generally among men in America—abdication of their responsibility. The result? "My people—infants are their oppressors, and women rule over them. O my people, your guides mislead you and they have swallowed up the course of your paths" (v. 12). God hands down a multi-count indictment against his people:

> For Jerusalem has stumbled, and Judah has fallen, because their speech and their deeds are against the LORD, defying his glorious presence. For the look on their faces bears witness against them; they proclaim their sin like Sodom; they do not hide it. Woe to them! For they have brought evil on themselves. . . . The LORD has taken his place to contend; he stands

> to judge peoples. The LORD will enter into judgment
> with the elders and princes of his people: "It is you
> who have devoured the vineyard, the spoil of the
> poor is in your houses. What do you mean by crush-
> ing my people, by grinding the face of the poor?"
> declares the Lord GOD of hosts. (Isa. 3:8–9, 13–15)

Could the crisis we are seeing in America today be a result
of similar sins and God's judgment?

By this time, you may be thinking: *This is pretty depressing
stuff. Is there any hope?* Yes, there is! God longs for us to return
to him, to his purposes and his ways so that he can forgive and
heal (see 2 Chron. 7:14). Thankfully, our sinful culture does not
have the last word on manhood and true masculinity. God does.
In the Scriptures, we find life-giving solutions to the crisis of
manhood, starting with a biblical model of manhood. So hang
in there. Stay tuned—there's good news for you as a man! With
God, you can do this!

Toward a Solution

What does God intend for us as men? What is his design and
purpose for us? For that, we must go back to the beginning, back
to Genesis.

> Then God said, "Let us make man in our image, after
> our likeness. And let them have dominion over the
> fish of the sea and over the birds of the heavens and
> over the livestock and over all the earth and over
> every creeping thing that creeps on the earth." So God
> created man in his own image, in the image of God
> he created him; male and female he created them.
> And God blessed them. And God said to them, "Be
> fruitful and multiply and fill the earth and subdue it,

and have dominion over the fish of the sea and over
the birds of the heavens and over every living thing
that moves on the earth." (Gen. 1:26–28)

To be created in "his own image" means we are in many
ways a reflection of God. He was saying: "The man will be like
me, and unlike anything else I have created on earth. No other
earth-bound creature has a mind to know me, a will to obey me,
or a heart to love me. No other creature will have an eternal des-
tiny. No other creature will have dominion and rule."

When God created us in his image, he not only delegated
to us the responsibility to care for his creation as stewards of
the earth, he also gave us dominion. God's first command was
"be fruitful and multiply," but his second command was "rule."
That dominion extends to far more than superiority over animals; it involves taming the wilderness, harnessing its produce
and energy, discovering its intricacies in order to leverage them
for our benefit, etc. God endowed us with the responsibility to
manage what he made.

Indeed, our influence as image-bearers of God should hold
sway over all dimensions of creation and culture. That's why
Jesus referred to us as the "salt of the earth" and the "light of the
world" (Matt. 5:13–16). That's why he said to take the gospel to
the ends of the earth (Acts 1:8). That's why, when he returns, we
will completely fulfill this command to rule as his co-regents in
the age to come (Rev. 2:26–27). We were created to rule. A more
modern translation could be: "lead."

Created to Lead

While Genesis 1 gives the macro view, Genesis 2 offers a micro
view. The wide lens on "humankind" is exchanged for a zoom
lens, first on Adam and then Adam and Eve as a couple. Specifically, Genesis 2 gives us a picture of the man's delegated

authority to lead. "The LORD God took the man and put him in the garden of Eden to work it and keep it" (2:15). The Hebrew word translated "work" means just that: to work it, labor in it. With reference to a garden, it means to till, cultivate, and harvest it. Bottom line: God gave Adam a job. We all know about that. To *work* is part of our identity as men. From the produce of the land, Adam would be able to provide for those under his care. Our jobs enable us to do the same for those under our care. We also cultivate them, seeking God's help in trying to help them become all he has in mind for them.

But it was not only Adam's purpose to work, but also to *watch*. The Hebrew word translated "watch" means to keep, guard, protect, or have charge of. Every man is given a certain domain—his garden, if you will—to protect from threat. This points to Adam's leadership role as the defender or protector. So God delegated to Adam the privilege and responsibility of working in and watching over the garden. Consequently, provider and defender/protector are two major roles and responsibilities God has delegated to the man, and we will explore those separately and in depth in later chapters.

Also in Genesis 2, God gave Adam the responsibility to name the animals. Consider the profound implications of that responsibility of Adam as a leader. No animal, up to that point, had a name of its own. So God brings an animal with a great big, long neck. Adam says, "Yep, that's a giraffe." What else would you name something that looked like that? Then along came a skunk. And he said, "That's a skunk." What else would you call something that smelled like that? Once Adam named an animal, "that was its name" (2:19). God delegated to Adam real authority.

Then we read how God made Adam a companion, a "helper fit for him" and brought her to Adam (2:20–22). Notice God puts Adam to sleep and takes a rib and makes it into another living, breathing human being, a woman. As commentator

Matthew Henry says: "Not made out of his head to rule over him, nor out of his feet to be trampled upon by him, but out of his side to be equal with him, under his arm to be protected, and near his heart to be loved."[11] Why take a part of Adam? Why not start with a second lump of clay? The idea of completeness and unity is reinforced by God taking a part of man and making the woman. In fact, the Hebrew term for helper can even mean "second-self." They were originally one, and they could become one again in a new and better way.

When Adam woke up and saw Eve, look at what Adam says: "This at last is bone of my bones and flesh of my flesh; she shall be called Woman, because she was taken out of Man" (v. 23). The English versions don't really do it justice, but the Hebrew literally says: "Now, now at last, finally!" In fact, this phrase is the equivalent to an expletive. One Hebrew scholar said the best way to translate what Adam said when he saw Eve is, "WOW!" Adam had been looking at hippos and frogs and hogs, and then he sees Eve in all her natural beauty. No wonder he exploded with joy! Even after thousands of years of genetic defects, there's nothing like the beauty of a bride on her wedding day. I for one think that our man Adam may have been thinking of what lay ahead for himself and the woman in terms of intimacy, since that was part of God's design also.

Then Genesis 2:24–25 lays down the basics of marriage. We are to "leave and cleave" says the old King James Version. Marriage means as men we leave our parents and make a new family with our wife, and it is to be permanent. When we come together as husband and wife, we become "one flesh." Obviously, that means physical intimacy and leads to the fulfillment of God's first command to "be fruitful and multiply." What an amazing gift that is, right? But it means more than that. There is an emotional and spiritual oneness as well. Plus, these verses also tell us if God has not given you the gift of celibacy, then it is his will for you to marry. And the Bible says: "He who finds a wife finds a good thing and obtains favor from the LORD" (Prov. 18:22).

With reference to the authority God gave Adam as the leader, notice that Adam also named this companion "Woman" (v. 23). Now the original Hebrew word for woman in verse 23 comes from an Arabic root that means "to be soft." God built femininity into a woman. The Hebrew word for man comes from the root that means "to exercise power." God put masculinity in men. God put Adam to work taking care of the garden, and God put Eve to work bearing and nurturing children. Man is the protector and provider, and woman is the encourager and nurturer. God made us different. God made men to be men, and he made women to be women. We could say with the French folk: "*Vive la différence!*" Yet Adam, as he did with the animals, gave this companion God brought to him a name (see 3:20), which again was a demonstration of his authority.

It is also important to note that Adam's authority was not unlimited. God told him he was free to eat from any of the trees of the garden, save one, establishing the fact for Adam that God is the ultimate authority. God rules over all; therefore he makes the rules, and the rule was: "But of the tree of the knowledge of good and evil you shall not eat, for in the day that you eat of it you shall surely die" (2:16–17). Adam had to pass on that information to Eve, the wife God made from him and for him. That highlights another major role of every man, and that is instructor or teacher. Again, we will explore that role separately in a coming study, but back to that forbidden tree.

We all know the story. As Genesis 3:1–7 unfolds, Satan slithers into the garden, strikes up a conversation with Eve, who is apparently standing near the forbidden tree, and convinces her to rebel against God's clearly stated rule. Interestingly, Satan tempted Eve. She initially ate the fruit. But in verses 8–9, God calls for Adam. God holds the man responsible. As you are reading this, you might protest: "Wait a minute. Didn't Eve eat the fruit first? So why didn't God call *her* out?" Yes, she did, but God called out Adam instead of his wife, because God assigned Adam as his representative to carry out his agenda in the garden—working in it and watching over it—and as such he was uniquely accountable. Regardless of what Eve did, she did so under Adam's authority and leadership . . . or in this case, his lack of leadership. (Remember as a defender/protector, a man must protect those he loves even from ungodly choices in life. We will explore this more in chapters 2 and 4.)

This points to another basic role every man has in the home, and that is the priest, the chaplain, the spiritual leader. We are accountable to God for those in our spiritual oversight and care. That's why God called him out.

Again, someone might protest: "Give Adam a break, he can't be on guard 24/7. He wasn't there when the deed went down with the devil. How can he be held responsible?" Well, Bible school pictorial renderings of Genesis 3 don't necessarily reflect biblical truth. The truth is that Adam *was there* when it went down. Read 3:6 again and you find: ". . . She took of its fruit and ate, and she also gave some to her husband who was with her, and he ate." Adam was standing there the whole time! Eve's dialogue with the devil played out right before his eyes and ears, but Adam didn't make a peep of protest. He failed to protect Eve against the enemy. Even when Eve turned and handed him the fruit, Adam didn't object. Like an obedient beast, he just ate it. When Adam did this, he effectively abdicated his role as the leader of the home, and Eve assumed that role.

Don't miss this. God looked to Adam to defend the domain delegated to him. Adam was in charge. He was the leader. Yet Adam heard the devil's seductive pitch that straight-up contradicted what God told him to begin with, and yet he said and did nothing! Unfortunately, that is the pattern for most men today, who say and do little to defend their families from the devil's destructive deceptions. This pattern is due largely to the feminization of men we have already discussed, including demonizing the concept of "masculinity." Bottom line: this was a massive failure of leadership on Adam's part.

When Adam and Eve first felt their guilt from their sin, they covered themselves (v. 7). When they heard God coming, they hid (v. 8). And when God confronted Adam for this whole mess, he blamed his wife. But he did something even worse. By implication, he blamed God. This "good thing" God gave him was the reason he blew it, he said (v. 12). Adam failed to embrace his God-given identity and carry out his charge as ruler of the domain God gave him. Abdicating his authority, he became the follower instead of the leader. And when his God-given responsibility finally caught up with him, he resorted to blame. Today men blame their wives, their parents, their environment, whatever it is—just fill in the blank—rather than own up to the fact they failed to assume their God-given identity. They relinquished their right to rule. They failed to lead. And the result, as we saw cited in statistic after statistic, is disastrous.

Come on, brothers, since God gives us the authority to lead, he holds us accountable when we don't. He expects us to rule in concert with his commands and in submission to his ultimate rule as Lord. But he allows us the freedom to choose. For our love and worship of God to be real, it must be freely chosen, but the risk of God granting free choice is the possibility we might choose to rebel and sin against God. Notice God didn't stop Eve from being deceived or Adam from joining her in rebellion, and everything in their world (and ours) was turned upside down as a result.

Read Genesis 3:16–19, 22–24. Consider how dramatically Adam's situation changed. What started as work now became toil. What started as a breeze now became a battle. Everything changed for Adam with his work and his wife, even his home.

God sent Adam and Eve out of the garden. Adam had been given a domain to manage. When he failed, his entire domain was altered. The same is true today. Our decisions directly affect our dominion. All that is under our care and supervision is dramatically impacted when we fail to lead.

But here's the good news—the reverse is also true! When we as men accept our God-given responsibility to lead, when we rule our domains in alignment with his rule, when we care for those who are under our charge according to his commands, our domains are dramatically impacted for the good. When God created the world and everything in it, before sin entered the world and everything went sideways, he called it "good"; but when he created humankind, he proclaimed it "very good." When man follows God's design and purpose, it is very good. As a man, you're responsible to lead. You were created to lead. When you do, good things happen in your life and in the lives of those for whom you are responsible.

When Men Lead, Positive Results Follow

You might say: "Following God's plan and purpose for me sounds nice, but will it really help me in the real world?" Absolutely! According to research conducted by Dr. Pat Fagan and the Marriage and Religion Research Institute (MARRI), in concert with the Family Research Council, federal surveys clearly demonstrate that the man who gets married, stays married, and whose family worships weekly in a church yields the most favorable social outcomes in life. Compared to the non-intact family that worships less than monthly or never, national data illustrates the superiority in the following areas:[12]

Benefits for the Individual

- Happiness: 50% more likely to be happy in a general sense

- Performance: A third more likely to take pride in their work (34%)
- Health: Nearly a third more likely to rate their health excellent or very good (30%)

(From *The Case for Marriage*[13])

Benefits for a Married Couple

- Marital Satisfaction: 25% happier in their relationship
- Divorce or Separation: 50% less likely
- Adultery: More than four times less likely (7.7% vs. 33.8%)
- Earned Income: As much as five times more annually ($54K vs. $9.4K)

Benefits for Their Children

- Average High School GPA (English and Math): Almost half a grade point higher (2.94 vs. 2.48)
- Expulsion or Suspension from School: Nearly three times less likely
- Repeating a Grade: Nearly six times less likely (6% vs. 34%)
- Hard Drug Use: Nearly 2.5 times less likely (8.5% vs. 20.1%)
- Drunkenness: Nearly two times less likely (22.4% vs. 41.2%)
- Same-Sex Activity: Three times less likely (2.5% vs. 7.5%)
- Running Away from Home: Over 2.5 times less likely
- Average Number of Sex Partners (Females): Over three times less (0.47 vs. 1.55)

In addition, fathers make a tremendous difference in the spiritual lives of their children:

- If a child is the first person in a household to become a Christian, there is a 3.5% probability everyone else in the household will follow.
- If the mother is the first to become a Christian, there is a 17% probability everyone else in the household will follow.

- If the father is first, there is a 93% probability everyone else in the household will follow.[14]

The statistics don't lie. There is a better way, and God's way works! He wants to help men lead healthy, successful, fulfilling lives, marriages, and families. The future of America depends on it!

Background on Joshua—"God's General"

Just think about the awesome responsibility that was thrust on Joshua. He grew up as a slave in Egypt. As a young man, the only thing he knew was back-breaking, soul-crushing work, making bricks and constructing monuments for the Egyptian overlords. Day after grueling day, Joshua had experienced unrelenting heat, unquenchable thirst, extreme exhaustion, and the sting of a taskmaster's whip. Enter Moses, God's appointed leader. Ten plagues later, God miraculously delivered Moses, Joshua, and the Hebrew people from Egyptian slavery. Thus began their journey out of Egypt and to the land God promised them. There were many challenges along the way, first from Pharaoh's armies and an uncrossable Red Sea, then an absence of food and water and the presence of enemies; but God came through every time with Moses as their leader.

For forty years it had been Joshua's honor to serve as an assistant and walk in the footsteps of Moses, the great man of God. What a life Moses lived! The baby whom God protected from Pharaoh's death sentence on Hebrew boys; the prince of Egypt; the desert shepherd; the man of God who walked into the court of Pharaoh and demanded: "Let my people go"; the man who had met God face to face and received the Ten Commandments; the man who led the people through the wilderness, interceding on behalf of the people—then the great man of God announced he was going to die. What a shock that must have been to Joshua!

I'm sure he fully expected Moses to lead the people into Canaan. It is difficult to imagine what must have raced through Joshua's mind in response to the enormity of the task now given to him.

Moses said to Joshua in his farewell address:

> "I am 120 years old today. I am no longer able to go out and come in. The LORD has said to me, 'You shall not go over this Jordan.'" . . . Then Moses summoned Joshua and said to him in the sight of all Israel, "Be strong and courageous, for you shall go with this people into the land that the LORD has sworn to their fathers to give them, and you shall put them in possession of it. It is the LORD who goes before you. He will be with you; he will not leave you or forsake you. Do not fear or be dismayed." (Deut. 31:2, 7–8)

Then the dreaded day came when what was predicted came true. Five words from the Lord filled Joshua and the hearts of the Hebrew people with anxiety: "Moses my servant is dead" (Josh. 1:2). Now Moses was gone. He was their security blanket, and the whole nation must have been filled with unease about the future, including Joshua. No more manna, no more pillar of cloud or fire to guide them. Now they had to begin again.

The Israelites had never been in a place like they were now. God had lifted the curse that had been upon them because of their unbelief. They had wandered in circles in the wilderness for forty years, and they were now on the edge of the land of promise; and God had told them to go into that land, not only to settle it, but to destroy all its inhabitants. So here is Joshua and the Hebrew people on the threshold of that awesome assignment.

Honestly, Joshua had little military experience, commanding only one major battle against the Amalekites during their time in the wilderness (Exod. 17:8–16). The Israelites had primarily been nomads over the past generation; they had few weapons to speak of, and God commanded them to conquer a land inhabited by seven of the fiercest tribes of people in that part of the world—tribes known for their size, their military expertise, their advanced weaponry (e.g., chariots of iron in Josh. 17:16), and their fortified cities. Talk about a challenge! It must have weighed on Joshua like a ton of Egyptian bricks! But Joshua became "God's General," leading the Israelites into future battles with the strength and courage only God could provide.

And so it is for us as men. We have plenty of challenges before us. Being a man in our day is no easy thing. The education complex has skewed standards and testing away from the way we process mentally, making it more difficult for us to make the grade. Colleges and the culture want you to rid yourself of "toxic masculinity," to reprogram you to be less male. Businesses are under pressure to advance women over men. Hollywood portrays you as slow and inferior, needing to be rescued. So when men don't measure up, it's almost like a self-fulfilling prophecy. The odds are stacked against us. And if the first study didn't contain enough statistical data to prove it, you have your own experience.

In fact, leave aside the challenges presented by culture and simply focus on your life. There are plenty coming at us at every age and stage of life: from settling questions about faith, getting through school, learning a trade, finding a job and succeeding in it, navigating romantic relationships, getting married and staying married, buying and maintaining a home, raising kids and paying for their education, blending families and making it work, rekindling your marriage and avoiding infidelity, recovering from a job loss or financial setbacks, saving money and planning for retirement, battling with health problems, dealing with the death of a loved one or spouse—these and many more challenges greet us every day as men.

Strong and Courageous

How can we rise to meet those challenges? How can we fulfill our God-given calling to lead well and successfully care for those under our charge? Well, let's go back to the book of Joshua for the answers. Remember, Joshua was a man like you. Don't make the mistake of looking at him as some stained-glass saint, sword raised triumphantly. In the face of all the challenges that confronted Joshua as the newly installed leader, he must have been intimidated. He must have been fearful. How do we know? Because of what God said to him over and over at the beginning:

> "No man shall be able to stand before you all the days of your life. Just as I was with Moses, so I will be with you. I will not leave you or forsake you. Be strong and courageous, for you shall cause this people to inherit the land that I swore to their fathers to give them. Only be strong and very courageous, being careful to do according to all the law that Moses my servant commanded you. Do not turn from it to the right hand or to the left, that you may have good success wherever you go.... Have I not commanded you? Be strong and courageous. Do not be frightened, and do not be dismayed, for the LORD your God is with you wherever you go." (Josh. 1:5–7, 9)

Three times the Lord tells Joshua: "Be strong and courageous!" And if that was not enough, when Joshua took command, the Hebrew people saluted him as their new leader and replied, you guessed it: "Only be strong and courageous" (Josh. 1:18). The Hebrew word for "be strong" means to be resolute and rigid, fortified and firm. It is the same word Samson used when he prayed: "Strengthen me only this once, O God," and

God empowered him to topple that pagan Philistine temple (Judg. 16:28). It can also mean to "grab hold." That's how it is used in Isaiah 42:6: "I am the LORD; I have called you in righteousness; I will take you *by the hand* and keep you" (emphasis added). God is saying: "Joshua, grab hold of me, and I will be your strength!" Then he added: "and be courageous." The word means to be brave and bold. Someone has said that "courage is not the absence of fear but the presence of faith." Being courageous starts with a mindset that launches you in the direction of your challenge with the will to prevail.

Why could God call on Joshua to be strong and courageous in view of all the impossible-looking challenges before him? Because God promised: "No one will be able to stand against you as long as you live. For I will be with you, just as I was with Moses. I will not fail you or abandon you. . . . Do not be afraid or discouraged. For the LORD your God is with you wherever you go" (Josh. 1:5, 9 NLT). Without God? Impossible. With God? Victory! What a promise! And what God told Joshua three times in the first chapter is what you need to hear in view of your challenges as a man: "Be strong and courageous!"

Notice not only dependence on God but obedience to God: "Only be strong and very courageous, *being careful* to do according to all the law that Moses my servant commanded you" (1:7, emphasis added). The place to start is here: absolute dependence on and obedience to God. There is no substitute. There is no shortcut. Learning that simple truth is hard. But that is what the men's ministry Stand Courageous is all about—helping men develop character, cultivate habits, build relationships, and make commitments that will move us closer to God's good purpose and design, men who will Stand Courageous!

BATTLE BUDDY GROUP GUIDE

Week 1 – Men Needed

▶ Every Man Needs a Transcendent Cause
LTG (RET.) Jerry Boykin from his book *Man to Man*

In 1993 in Mogadishu, Somalia, I was the Delta Force commander during the events that are most commonly referred to as "Black Hawk Down." Two Black Hawk helicopters were shot down in the city of five million people, where most of those people were starving refugees. Within thirty minutes of the first chopper being shot down, the second one was shot down.

When the first chopper went down, I sent every one of my soldiers who were already fighting in the city to the rescue of the crew and passengers of that first crash. I was left with few options when the second helo went down over a mile away from the first crash. I had to pull together a second rescue effort using those soldiers, sailors, and airmen who were left in the base—many of whom were not from the combat arms specialties (they were clerks, mechanics, communicators, and supply people). To their credit, every man was eager to be part of the effort to rescue their brothers at the second crash site.

Two of the Delta Force snipers, Randy Shughart and Gary Gordon, watched the second Black Hawk go down from their position in another helo. The Black Hawk helicopter carrying Shughart and Gordon was being used as an airborne sniper platform. They radioed immediately to inform us that the crew in the second crash was alive but injured, and it appeared that they could not get themselves out of their seats. They reported, "Their backs are probably broken. Put us in and we can get them out."

The answer was immediate. "We can't send you in because we have nobody to support you with. You would be going into a hornet's nest since everybody's at the first crash site. It'll take a while to get a force together to send in there to help you out. Stay above them and keep shooting—take out as many Somalis as you can."

They did. But they called back in less than thirty minutes and said, "There are too many Somalis coming in. You've got to put us on the ground!"

The answer was "No" for the second time.

The third time they called they sounded both adamant and desperate, "We're the only hope; put us in."

It was important to question their situational awareness regarding what was happening. Did they fully understand the risks? They reported that they were well aware of what they would be going into since they were watching it unfold from their perch in the helo.

"Yes, put us in." They went in. And they fought valiantly, but both gave their lives to save one of their own.

The lone survivor from the crash told us the incredible story of Randy and Gordy, which became the narrative for the recommendations for the Medals of Honor for both men. Chief Warrant Officer Michael Durant, the pilot of the crashed bird, relayed the following story.

The two snipers jumped to the ground from a lower hover of their Black Hawk and began firing on Somali militia as they fought their way into the crash site. Once at the crash site, Randy covered Gordy as Gordy helped the four crew members out of the crash. Once he had them out of the helo, he helped them to find cover between the crash and a stone wall next to it.

Task accomplished, Gordy moved around the helo to help Randy engage the Somali militia determined to get to the crash. Both snipers were putting out a pretty heavy volume of fire, according to Chief Durant, until Gordy came back around to his side of the helo and asked if there was more ammo in the crashed chopper. When Durant told him to look behind the co-pilot seat, Gordy retrieved the supply and returned to Durant with a fully loaded MP5 submachine gun, laid it on Durant's chest, and said, "good luck" before returning to the side where Randy was still engaging targets.

Gordy tossed ammo to Randy, who reloaded and continued firing. Moments later, Durant heard Randy yell over to his teammate, "Gordy, I'm hit." His gun went silent quickly after he yelled to Gordy, and Mike Durant knew that Randy Shughart was most likely dead.

Only a few minutes passed before Gordy yelled in a feeble voice to Durant that he was hit also, and soon it was obvious that he, too, was dead. As the Somali militia swept over the crash site, they killed three of the four crew members, leaving only Chief Durant to tell the story.

I had the honor of standing in the West Wing of the White House as the U.S. president presented the medals to the widows and families of these two incredible warriors.

There is no question that those two men knew they were putting their lives on the line by going into that chaotic scene. Their request had been denied twice. Yet they still asked to go in. Why?

The answer is because they had a transcendent cause.

And what was that transcendent cause? In their case, it was part of the fifth stanza of the Ranger Creed: "Never shall I leave a fallen comrade to fall into the hands of the enemy." Those two men lived and died by it.[15] ◀

Group Debrief

General Boykin raised the issue of the "transcendent cause" with a riveting real-life story from what we know as "Black Hawk Down." He goes on to say:

> The question for today is this—have we assessed our lives to determine who and what it is that's worth living and dying for? One can be part of today's "give me" generation, or one can be part of "I'll give to you." Shughart and Gordon were givers—not takers. And they gave their lives. But they gave their lives because they had a transcendent cause. Their cause was—at the tactical level—the same for every warrior who's ever been on the battlefield: the guy behind you, next to you, and on your right and left.

Jesus came not as a taker but as a giver, as a servant who gave his life to liberate us. He took our place and our punishment on a cross and offers instead forgiveness and fullness of life for those who follow him. You were his "transcendent cause"! He told his disciples before his death:

> Jesus called them over and said to them, "You know that those who are regarded as rulers of the Gentiles lord it over them, and those in high positions act as tyrants over them. But it is not so among you. On the contrary, whoever wants to become great among you will be your servant, and whoever wants to be first among you will be a slave to all. For even the Son of Man did not come to be served, but to serve, and to give his life as a ransom for many." (Mark 10:42–45 csb)

Questions to Consider

- Who and what are you willing to die for? What is your transcendent cause?

- How does what Jesus did for us on the cross impact your transcendent cause?

- In your family context, would you judge yourself to be more of a giver or more of a taker?

- As the leader in your home, would your family consider you more of a "lord" or more of a "servant"?

CHAPTER 2

Man as a Provider

In Genesis, we learn one of the basic God-given roles and responsibilities for men is that of provider. God gave Adam the responsibility to "work" the garden (Gen. 2:15). From working the land, Adam could provide food for Eve and eventually his sons. Our jobs enable us to do the same for those under our care. Yet a man is to provide much more than money to secure the basics to physically sustain his family. The book of Joshua covers not only the basic role, but the other areas where men are to be providers. A critical area is that of providing direction.

Devotion to Direction – Joshua 1:1–9

It would be dark soon. My (Cureton's) wife was growing more anxious by the minute. We were on our first vacation, and we were lost and now stuck. I had foolishly driven our tiny two-door Honda Civic onto an unmarked dirt and gravel road in between Grand Teton and Yellowstone National Parks in search of a lake that promised trophy trout. Predictably, the road forked, but I couldn't find that on my paper map. Of course, there was no cell coverage. I needed help, but being a typical man, I decided I knew which way to take simply by male instinct. And yes, I took us in the wrong direction.

I drove that little car farther on an increasingly rough road, and the ruts got deeper and the rocks got bigger. We were scraping bottom, and my wife began to panic. Predictably, I kept pressing on into the woods in the wrong direction. We topped a steep hill and I saw the blue green lake in the distance, but this gravel road was taking us farther away from it. I stopped the car, mused that the road probably winds around to the lake. After all, I had big trout on the brain. I was like Daniel Boone, the great pioneer woodsman, who once famously said, "I can't say I was ever lost, but I was bewildered once for three days."[1]

Well, my wife was not amused, and offered her clear-eyed assessment: "Honey, we're lost. We've got to turn around; if you go down this hill, we may never make it back up in this little car." You guessed it. I proceeded down the steep hill, half skidding, half sliding. We made it to the bottom in a cloud of dust, but my wife was convinced we would never make it out unless we hiked. Challenge accepted. My mission for trout was set aside to prove I could get us back up that hill. We made it halfway up, and the little four-cylinder Civic dug in and spun its front wheels, rocks and gravel flying everywhere, dust billowing, engine at the redline. We stalled out halfway up.

So I backed the car down the hill and tried another approach with more speed. Same result. I backed down to the bottom of the hill and we considered our options. My wife was frantic. The sun was setting and shadows covered the valley. We were in the middle of grizzly country. The thought of having to spend the night out there put her over the edge. I prayed and she cried. I backed up the little Civic further and floored it. We made it halfway up when it began to bog down, but providentially, I turned the wheel and found more solid ground and we kept going, slowly but surely, up that hill until we made it to the top—by the grace of God! And yes, we praised God all the way back to our humble abode in the tent cabins at Colter Bay Village. But we never would have been in such a tight spot if I had not taken us in the wrong direction.

As a man, you are the primary provider of one of the key things your family needs: direction. And not just any direction, the *right* direction. It is difficult to admit we need help in this area, but we do. In Joshua 1:1–8, we find that God graciously provides us with direction. At this point in the Bible, Moses had just died and that was a big deal. For forty years they had the routine down out there in the wilderness, but things were going to change. Now they were about to start all over again with a new leader in a new land. But even Joshua must have been fearful about the future, because God told him three times here: "Be strong and courageous" (vv. 6, 7, 9).

Israel was poised on the very threshold of this awesome assignment to take the land, and God gives them a wonderful promise to lift their hearts, the promise of victory: "Every place that the sole of your foot will tread upon I have given to you, just as I promised to Moses" (v. 3). Notice it is past tense. It's a done deal. You say: "Wait a minute, they weren't even in the land yet. They haven't even crossed the Jordan yet." And yet God said, "I've *already* given it to you. The victory is yours!" God follows that promise with an even greater one to calm their fears, the promise of his presence: "No man shall be able to stand before you all the days of your life. Just as I was with Moses, so I will be with you. I will not leave you or forsake you" (v. 5). And just to make sure Joshua got it, he repeats it: "Have I not commanded you? Be strong and courageous. Do not be frightened, and do not be dismayed, for the Lord your God is with you wherever you go" (v. 9).

God references the land and even marks off the boundaries and tells them he has already given it to them. But then God gives Joshua, the leader, divine direction in verses 7–8:

"Only be strong and very courageous, being careful to do according to all the law that Moses my servant commanded you. Do not turn from it to the right hand or to the left, that you may have good success wherever you go. This Book of the Law shall not depart from your mouth, but you shall meditate on it day and night, so that you may be careful to do according to all that is written in it. For then you will make your way prosperous, and then you will have good success."

Regarding the law passed down through Moses, God is saying to Joshua, "This is your instruction manual that will be your guide. This will provide direction." The key to giving direction is all wrapped up in the Word of God. In order to provide your family with direction, you need to consult that manual. And there is a promise for those who do as God commands: "For then you will make your way prosperous, and then you will have good success."

But before we get to the promise, let's make sure we meet the conditions. God had three requirements for Joshua and for us if we want to enjoy the kind of success he intends for us:

1. The Word of God is to be in our mouth: In other words, we are to verbalize the Word of God. We are to speak it, not just read it. Not just memorize it. We should verbalize it in order to vitalize it, to make it real. There is something very powerful about taking God's words and speaking them.

When Jesus was tempted in the wilderness, Satan tried to deceive and destroy him three times. Jesus responded three times, verbalizing the Word of God (Matt. 4:1–11). He quoted Deuteronomy 8:3, then 6:16, and finally 6:13. Jesus took God's Word from the law Moses handed to Joshua and spoke it to

Satan, and Satan was defeated! Learn to speak God's Word, not only to overcome temptation, but to provide direction. Remember, the psalmist said, "Your word is a lamp to my feet and a light to my path" (Ps. 119:105).

For example, the Bible tells us God's will is our sanctification, that we increasingly become more and more like Jesus (1 Thess. 4:3–4). The first step is to "abstain from sexual immorality." So tell your family out loud: "Avoid sexual immorality." Knowing they are going to be tempted, tell them when they go to school or work or on a date or are just hanging out or surfing the web: "Avoid sexual immorality." Here's another one: "Abstain from every form of evil" (1 Thess. 5:22). My dad used to quote this to me and it stuck. When my buddies suggested some questionable activity on the weekend, my dad's voice replayed in my head, and it kept me out of a lot of trouble. Take the Word of God and put it in your mouth to provide direction.

We speak about Facebook posts, football games, food, and finance—everything in the world but the Word of God. But if you want to enjoy success as a man who leads, God's Word needs to be in your mouth. Moses said concerning the laws of God, "You shall teach them diligently to your children, and shall talk of them when you sit in your house, and when you walk by the way, and when you lie down, and when you rise" (Deut. 6:7; 11:19). Not only should God's Word be in your mouth, it needs to be in your mind.

2. The Word of God needs to be in your mind: Look at verse 8 again: "you shall meditate on it day and night." The original Hebrew word "meditate" has in it the idea of humming. The Word of God is to be like a tune that gets stuck in your head. Have you ever heard some song in the morning, and then you find yourself humming it all day long? That's the idea of meditating on the Word of God. The Lord commanded, "You shall therefore lay up these words of mine in your heart and in your soul" (Deut. 11:18). The Hebrew word translated "imprint" (or "impress" KJV) can mean to plant, to mark, or to fix something in place. So clear a spot and plant the Word of God in your mind. Take a mallet and drive it in, or a hammer and nail it in like a sign you can't miss. Fix it in your mind, think about it, meditate on it. Yes, even memorize it. Otherwise, how are you going to speak it?

Senator Daniel Webster was one of the greatest American orators, and one of the secrets of his great oratorical skill was his practice of reciting the Word of God. Yet to recite it, he had to memorize it, which he did from his youth. School Master James Tappan, one of Daniel's first school teachers, told the story of how Daniel received his first pocket knife:

> Daniel was always the brightest boy in the school. . . . He would learn more in five minutes than any other boy in five hours. . . . One Saturday, I remember, I held up a handsome new jackknife to the scholars and said the boy who would commit to memory the greatest number of verses in the Bible by Monday morning should have it. Many of the boys did well; but when it came to Daniel's turn to recite, I found that he had committed so much [to memory] that after hearing him repeat some sixty or seventy verses, I was obliged to give up, he telling me that there were several chapters yet that he had learned. Daniel got that jackknife.[2]

Senator Daniel Webster used a knife to carve his name in his desk in the U.S. Senate; and if you go on a tour of the U.S. Capitol, you can see that very desk today, and every senior senator from New Hampshire gets to carve his or her name in Senator

Webster's old desk. But the way he made his true mark was by memorizing and speaking the Word of God. Now I know what you are thinking: *Me, memorize chapters of the Bible?* I hear you, but don't tune out just yet. Try starting with one verse a week. Enter it as a note on your phone and review it. Put it on a sticky note and put it on your mirror you use in the morning and say it out loud every day.

Ask God: "What are you saying to me? What does that mean? How does this apply to me? What does this mean for my family and the direction we should go?" Hopefully by the end of the week it will be a part of you. And then you can impart it to your family to provide direction.

So the Word of God is to be in your mouth and on your mind. That's the second key to success in having what you need to provide direction. Here's the third key: the Word of God should be in your manners—that is, your behavior, the way you act, your conduct.

3. The Word of God is to be in your manners: Look back at verse 8: "so that you may be careful to do according to all that is written in it." That means to meditate on God's Word with the purpose of obeying it. See, Bible study and meditation doesn't really give you knowledge of God. Bible study gives you knowledge about God, but obedience gives you knowledge *of* God. Jesus said, "Whoever has my commandments and keeps them, he it is who loves me. And he who loves me will be loved by my Father, and I will love him and manifest myself to him" (John 14:21). As one of my mentors, Dr. Henry Blackaby, puts it: "You come to know God by experience as you obey Him."[3] And when you obey, Jesus will become real to you! When you obey, the Bible will literally come alive with meaning, purpose, and direction. It should change your character and your conduct. Consequently, you're not just to read the Bible simply for information, but ultimately for transformation. It is to change your way of life! You are to read it and study it so that you can do it!

Turn to God's Word for direction when . . .

- You are lost and confused
- You need to make a decision about a degree plan or a career
- You are unsure of a romantic relationship
- Your marriage is on the rocks
- You don't know how to talk with your teen
- You have a terminally ill spouse or parent

Turn to God's Word for direction. We ought to pray every day as we open the Bible, "Lord, show me today what you want me to do. Show me how to conform my life to your will and your ways. Lord, I commit myself today that whatever you say to me I will do it with your help. Whatever direction you send me, there I will go. And God, help me give my family your direction." That's what we ought to pray as we open the Word of God daily. Expect God's direction not only for your life but also for your marriage, children, grandchildren, church service, career, citizenship, etc. Citizenship? Yes, God's Word even provides direction on how to vote! Let God's Word guide you in every area of life!

Notice God says: "Do not turn from it to the right hand or to the left" (v. 7). In other words, stay on course. In 2018, the *Dallas Morning News* reported a tragedy of a man who went off course. Officials say the pilot of a small Texas-bound aircraft diverted from his original flight plan and crashed into the Gulf of Mexico. The pilot was identified as fifty-five-year-old Bill Kinsinger of Edmond, Oklahoma, an anesthesiologist who volunteered to fly rescue animals. According to the FAA, his Cirrus SR22T left Wiley Post Airport in Oklahoma City and was to land in Georgetown, Texas, to pick up a rescue dog but did not make it.

Far off course from his flight plan, the North American Aerospace Defense Command sent two F-16 fighter jets from Houston to make contact with the plane after its pilot stopped responding to instructions from air-traffic control. The jets dropped flares and flew in front of the plane to get the pilot's attention, but the pilot did not respond and the plane continued off course. The pilot finally went off the radar, and it is presumed he crashed in the Gulf. Best Fur Friends Rescue in Fort Worth posted on Facebook about Kinsinger: "We are just devastated and are sending the most heartfelt prayers to his family and all those who love him."[4] Sadly, this man veered off course, missed his destination, and ultimately crashed. What a tragedy.

The message: stay on course. Don't turn to the right or the left from the direction found in God's Word. Many men go off course and they crash and burn. We all know someone who fits that description. Maybe you've been there. But the good news is that you can course-correct. You can get on track and stay on track. Plus, if you stay on course, you are more likely to keep those in your charge on course. Don't make detours. Make the Word of God your compass, and you will provide direction for those in your care.

Really that's how to define success: obey God. Let the Word of God be in your mouth, on your mind, dictate your manner of life, your behavior, and your conduct. Live it out by putting God's Word in action. Your family will see your walk matches your talk.

My mother, Gwen Boykin, was a woman who read and studied the Word every day, even though she did not have a high school diploma. Throughout her last decade on earth, she was afflicted with Alzheimer's disease and could not speak, nor did she recognize anyone. When she lay dying, she was mumbling what appeared to be just gibberish. My sister-in-law went to her bedside and leaned down close to her for a moment. When she arose from my mother's side, she smiled and stated to all in the room, "She is quoting Scripture," and indeed she was. Her spirit was not afflicted with the terrible disease, and clearly God was reminding her of all his promises. That is what we men have to do: read the Word, memorize key Scriptures, and speak what we have learned, keeping the Word in our mouths. Then we can provide direction to those in our families as well as the people we influence. We cannot find excuses for not filling our mind and heart with Scripture if we sincerely want to be the man that we are called to be.

Check the statement that describes the current role of God's Word in your life:

- I read it every day and depend on it as my source of life.
- I read it every chance I get.
- I use it to get guidance when problems arise.
- I read it during my small-group Bible study.
- Other

Pray

God, make me a man of your Word. May your Word be in my mouth as I speak. May your Word be in my mind as I make decisions. May your Word mark my manner of life, my behavior, my conduct. Lead me by your Word as I lead those whom you have entrusted to me to provide direction.

The Worth of Work – Joshua 1:10–18

My dad (Cureton's) taught me the worth of work. He was a hard-working man who progressed his way up from an hourly worker to being the number three man in the company, which was eventually bought out by BASF, a big chemicals company.

Through his hard work, my dad provided for our family, and he expected us to work as well. So on my sixteenth birthday, I went into a local grocery store that was hiring clerks or "bag boys," who put groceries into paper sacks for customers. I got the job and started that day. Now I had already been working for years doing all kinds of jobs as a kid, from mowing grass, loading hay bales, suckering tobacco, raking leaves, etc.; but in my state, official employment began at sixteen and I started on day one. That job has mostly been replaced by the DIY checkout stations, but we were full service, helping those who needed to get their groceries loaded in their vehicles. We also had to gather grocery carts and push them back up the hill into the store, stock shelves, sweep and mop, clean the customer bathrooms, and work in the returnable pop bottles. I worked there seven years through high school and college, during which I graduated to running a register and checking in vendors at the loading dock. After I got married, we moved to Texas for seminary, and I worked in warehouses and pastored a small church on weekends. Except for moving for six months of study in Sweden when I was working on my dissertation, I have been continuously employed ever since.

As men, we are wired to work. We are made to make. We are geared to generate. It is part of the image of God, who sets the example as Creator and Provider. Jesus said, "My Father is working until now, and I am working" (John 5:17). While Jesus is referring to his mission, he was also a working man. Honestly, the pictures of Jesus that used to grace our Sunday school classrooms when I was growing up—depicting Jesus with long, flowing golden brown hair, looking like a "Breck Girl" commercial—are mistaken at best and misleading at worst. No, Jesus was a real man, a man's man.

Raised in a blue-collar home, Jesus took up Joseph's trade as a carpenter, a builder. He worked with wood and stone. I imagine he had splinters in his fingers, calluses on his hands, a strong back, and a muscular build from physical labor. In fact, critics in Nazareth asked: "Is not this the carpenter . . . ?" (Mark 6:3). In the original language, the verb is in the present tense. So it is highly likely that Jesus was still working as a builder during the initial stages of his ministry of preaching, teaching, and healing. The apostle Paul apparently worked as a tentmaker to provide income so as not to be a burden while on his missionary journeys (1 Thess. 2:9). The point is this: part of our divinely assigned role as men is that we work to provide for ourselves and others. Obviously, some men have disabilities and can't work, while others have worked all their lives and have retired from their work. But for the rest of us, it is a regular part of who we are as men. Our work enables us to provide for those in our care, which is the basic role we are considering in this chapter.

For Joshua it was the same. Even though God had already given the promised land for the taking, there were many battles to fight, walls to bring down, and giants to kill. Joshua didn't just have to work for it, he had to go to *war* for it. Sometimes it meant following God's strange battle plans, like at Jericho where they marched around the city and blew trumpets; and yet they still had to go in and fight in the mop-up operation, defeating the enemy and securing the victory. Other times it was simply straight-up army against army, and that meant *mano a mano* fighting. It was muscle against muscle, spear against armor, sword against shield. It took a lot of praying and planning, marching and fighting. Suppose that Israel had stayed in the wilderness, never crossing the Jordan River or engaging the enemy. They would've never enjoyed what God had promised them. It would be like having the claim to a productive gold mine, but never actually going down in there to dig it up, haul it out, and cash it in. It takes work. One of the statements that really bothers me is one that I have too often said, "God is in control." I finally realized that for many people that phrase means, ". . . therefore I don't have to do anything." WRONG! God works through us in many situations, and working to see his promises fulfilled is an imperative for us, especially us men.

God knew Joshua would face some fierce enemies who would fight tooth and claw to stop him and the armies of Israel. Yet God preemptively promised: "No man shall be able to stand before you all the days of your life" (v. 5a). No matter how much Israel might have been intimidated by the cruelty of the Canaanites and the hostility of the Hittites or awestruck by the Anakim who towered over them, God said no one would be able to stand against them. They would be unstoppable. Why? God said, "Just as I was with Moses, so I will be with you. I will not leave you or forsake you" (v. 5b).

Basically, God said of Israel's enemies: "Resistance is futile!" Yet they did resist. And Joshua and his armies had to go out and fight. Bottom line: what was true for Joshua and the Israelites is also true for us today. God promises to provide and has already given us everything we need to succeed in obtaining that provision. He has put us in an environment with opportunities. He has given us skills and abilities. But also like Joshua, we have a part to play in realizing and actualizing what God has promised to provide for us. And that takes hard work.

First, Joshua issued orders (vv. 10–11) and reminded the two-and-a-half tribes who had already gotten their part of the promised land: "Your wives, your little ones, and your livestock shall remain in the land that Moses gave you beyond the Jordan, but all the men of valor among you shall pass over armed before your brothers and shall help them" (v. 14). Now this is interesting. These tribes already had their part of the promised land, yet they were expected to help the other tribes fight to get their share. Someone might say: "Why did they have to go out and fight? After all, these other tribes were not immediate family."

First of all, they had given Moses their word they would (see Numbers 32). Second, when part of the nation was at war, all the nation was at war. In fact, warriors from these two-and-a-half tribes had to march out in front and form the vanguard in the attack!

This is a good place to make a present-day application. As men, first of all we are to provide for our immediate families. In fact, Scripture warns: "But if anyone does not provide for his relatives, and especially for members of his household, he has denied the faith and is worse than an unbeliever" (1 Tim. 5:8). Need I say more? OK, I will. Being a provider of the physical needs of our families is a distinct part of our manhood and calling as delegated representatives of God the Father, who continually provides for our daily needs. While your wife may have a job and contribute to the overall financial stability of your family, you are still the primary provider. Yes, even if she has a better-paying job than you do, it is your God-given role and responsibility.

If you're divorced, you need to make sure you're still providing for your ex-wife and the kids you fathered. The fact that you are no longer married doesn't relieve you of your obligation of obeying God in your role as provider. If you have fallen behind in supporting your family, start praying about how you can sacrifice to catch up. Don't try to rationalize your way out of it. Just trust God, roll up your sleeves, and do it. Honestly, we could significantly reduce the welfare rolls and poverty level in this nation if more male "sperm donors" who abandoned the women they impregnated would offer to marry them, if possible, but at least attempt to be a father to their child, and start taking their role as provider seriously.

As we showed with research statistics on married families who worship together weekly doing better in every statistical category, the conclusion is that God's way works. So should you as a man. Work to provide for your wife and your children and your family.

If you want to find out how well you are doing as a provider, ask your wife and kids: "Do you feel like your needs are met? How can I do a better job of taking care of you? What makes you feel most secure? Are you confident that I love you and will always be there for you?" If your wife faints from shock, after she wakes up invite her to have an honest conversation, even make a list. Now this takes guts—kind of like daring a guy in school to hit you and you see the punch coming. Yet you need to know what they are thinking and feeling. You may be pleasantly surprised, or you may have some improvements to make. But know this, when you take seriously your responsibility as a provider, you will have a sense of fulfillment that only comes from obeying God. In addition, your family will grow in their respect and love for you; and when you have to make a tough decision that affects the family, you will have the credibility to lead, and it will be more likely that they will follow. So provide well for your family!

However, the point about the two-and-a-half tribes on the other side of the Jordan committing their forces to join the fight is this: there are also folks in need outside our family, and we can and should help them as God leads. Obviously, when you give God your tithe through your local church, your church is hopefully meeting not only spiritual but also physical needs, such as food, help with rent, medical bills, etc. There are other ministries and nonprofit organizations outside the church that specialize in helping people, and you might want to consider investing in them. Franklin Graham's Samaritan's Purse comes to mind, but there are many others. Additionally, there will be opportunities for you to personally meet a real need and alleviate suffering—Scripture is full of admonitions to do so.

But back to Joshua and his people preparing for war. Someone might ask, "If God wanted to give his people this land

flowing with milk and honey, why didn't he take out these enemies before Israel got there and let them walk in without a war?"
As you read the rest of the book, you'll find that God didn't
simply vaporize or otherwise vacate the evil people living in the
promised land. Instead, Joshua led the people into battle after
battle against these hostile heathen city-states, whose idolatrous
immorality demanded God's judgment in the harshest form of
all—death and displacement by the sword. But this whole process required blood, sweat, tears, and a lot of labor on the part of
Israel. If given a choice, no doubt they would have chosen for the
land to be vacant when they marched in, but that choice was not
available to them. There was only one way to occupy the land,
and that was to go to war.

Warfare is an intense form of work. And work is the normal
process of receiving God's provision and then passing it on to
those in our care. While sometimes God simply drops provision into our laps without us doing anything, most of the time
he graciously provides the environment, the opportunity, the
skill, and the strength so that we can work for it. When Jesus
told us not to worry by pointing to the birds and how our heavenly Father cares for them (Matt. 6:25–26), did he mean that
God drops worms into their mouths from a clear blue sky? Not
hardly! God provides the environment, opportunity, and ability,
and the birds go searching and scratching. They work hard to
get those worms. Then they go back to their nest and provide
for their brood with some food. It is no different for us as men.
Being a Christian man who provides is far from a call to pious
passivity. It is a call to industrious activity. It is a call to work.

When my (Cureton's) dad discovered he had terminal cancer,
just two years into an early retirement, his life verse became John
9:4 where Jesus said, "I must work the works of Him who sent
Me while it is day; the night is coming when no one can work"
(NKJV). My dad, who was often sick and got weaker by the day,

nevertheless won more people to faith in Christ during those two years than he did in all his previous years as a Christian. When "the night" came for Dad, he was at his most productive. Most guys reading this are not dying of terminal cancer. So get up off the couch and out of the recliner. Put down your game controller, tune out Twitter, and get your face out of Facebook. Stop whining, stop worrying, and start working! Roll up your sleeves, put your game face on, and go to work for what God has provided for you so that you can provide for your family and for others in need.

Pray

Loving Father, our Provider, thank you for graciously providing for our needs. Just as you provide for the "birds of the air," thank you for providing the environment and opportunity, the skill and strength to take full advantage of your providence and work to provide for our families and other folks in need. Lord, forgive us for being so pious that we become passive and thus tempted to shirk our responsibility as providers. May we follow the example of hard work and industry set for us by your Son, who worked all the way up until they nailed him to the cross, in whose name we pray, Amen.

The Importance of Identity – Joshua 5:1–12

Her name was Billie, and she was over ninety years old. It was the first time we had met by phone, but we shared something in common. We were both Curetons. She knew all about our family history, and as a young man with small kids, I wanted to know what she knew. When I was a kid, we took trips for holidays to visit my dad's family, and Dad would remind my sister and me of who we were and where we came from. For me back then, it was sort of like reading all the "begat" chapters in the Bible. It was mostly boring information, except for the occasional highlights, like the fact that my dad's grandmother on his mom's side was a full-blooded Cherokee or that one of our relatives was a lawman who chased other relatives who were moonshiners. Today, I'd give anything to hear my dad tell me about our family tree.

When I spoke with Billie, my dad had recently died of cancer, but before he passed he had started a more intensive search for our family history, visiting several county courthouses. His search ended prematurely with his death. But Billie had more intel than Dad did on our family tree, and she excitedly gave me a snapshot of our Cureton clan from a wide-angle lens. She had traced the family all the way back to the 1540s in Middlesex, England. Most Curetons were educated, part of the budding middle class, and Catholic, which made them the subject of persecution, depending on who was on the British throne. She told me about two Cureton brothers, who came over to North Carolina to survey for the royal governor in the 1740s, which brought them to what is now east Tennessee. In exchange for their services, they received land, and started a river ferry business in the same region where my father was born.

Billie related that eventually the Cureton clan in frontier America was swept up in the Second Great Awakening, becoming mostly Methodists and Baptists, but still valuing education, including for the young ladies. Now there are Curetons all over America of every faith and no faith at all, some uneducated and some highly educated. When I hung up with that dear lady, I didn't know it would be the last time we would speak before her death; but I did know I had to share what I learned from her with my wife and two children, in addition to the other things my dad showed me from his research before his death.

My youngest, Will, now grown, married, and carrying forward the Cureton name, occasionally asks me to rehearse our family history. In fact, we took his first name from his great-grandfather William (Bill) Steele, WWII Army veteran on my wife's side, and his great-grandfather William (Bill) McCravey, WWII Navy veteran on my mother's side. We took his middle name from my grandfather Fredrick (Fred) on my dad's side, but also from a British scholar active in the 1880s named William Fredrick Cureton, who discovered an ancient manuscript of the New Testament that bears our family name: Curetonian Syriac. We've told Will that his name means defender and protector, and he takes that very seriously. It is a part of his identity.

My eldest, Kristen, married to a seminary student, we named after Professor Birger Gerhardsson's wife Kirsten—the anglicized version. We first discovered Kristen was coming along when my wife and I were living in Denmark and I was working on my dissertation with Prof. Gerhardsson at the University of Lund in Sweden. In fact, Kristen calls herself our Danish child. But seriously, we told Kristen that her name means "follower of Christ" or "Christ-bearer." It is part of her identity. She is a bold "Christ-bearer" in the public schools. In fact, we talk about both sides of the family and each individual's devotion to the Christian faith, our family, and our freedom. That information gives our family a strong sense of identity, which is so important to provide in this crazy and confused world we live in today.

Obviously, fathers are critical to helping children affirm their God-created biology and matching identity as male and female. For example, biological males who "feel female" are going into ladies' bathrooms, locker rooms, showers, and participating in women's sports, not to mention having radical surgeries. Biological females are dressing and grooming like men as well as undergoing harsh hormone treatments. The result is brokenness and a lot of suicide. So men, step up and lead on this with those God has in your charge. Know that you will be going counter to the culture when you do, but you will be teaching them in alignment with the God who made us distinctly male and female (Gen. 1:27).

Dad, do not underestimate your incredible influence on your daughter and your son with regard to their respective identities. It is absolutely vital. They not only pick it up from your verbal and physical engagement with them, but also from the way you treat other women and interact with other men. They are always watching and listening and learning from you as an instructor. Treat your daughter like a princess. Do manly things with your son. Help them establish their identities. In many ways, the history of your family is the foundation of your identity. Hence, when that history is lost or impossible to discern, each man must begin to put together a proud legacy through his own actions and values that will one day provide a proud history for his posterity.

In Joshua 5, the people of God firmly reestablished their identity before going into their first battle against the walled city of Jericho. At this point, God had already miraculously stopped the raging river Jordan so Israel could cross. This chapter describes the consecration of the people of Israel in preparation for the military campaigns to defeat the hostile inhabitants of the land. For those of you who have served in combat, this chapter might seem to be a very strange way of preparing to go to war, especially from a man's point of view.

From all human appearances, this was the time to attack. God had given to Joshua, and Joshua had given to the people, God's promises of success and victory if they would but follow the direction of his word handed down through Moses. The people of Israel were no doubt filled with confidence after miraculously crossing the Jordan River on dry ground. Plus, intelligence reports came in that the enemy was demoralized and in disarray (5:1). Surely, it was time to launch the offensive. No doubt Joshua's tribal commanders must have been thinking, *It is go time, Joshua! The enemy is scared and shaking in his sandals! Let's do this!* Yet God's ways are higher than our ways. God said, "First things first. Follow the direction of my word!" To ensure victory, God required two observances from the law that reestablished their identity: submitting to circumcision and observing the Passover.

Submitting to Circumcision – Joshua 5:2–9

Admit it. Every self-respecting guy reading this at this point is recoiling a bit. But here it is in verse 2: "At that time the LORD said to Joshua, 'Make flint knives and circumcise the sons of Israel a second time.'" No surgical knives . . . no local anesthesia . . . no thank you, right? Yet verse 3 tells us the men of Israel stepped forward and submitted to being circumcised with crude flint knives at a place they named the "Hill of Foreskins." Can you imagine a son asking about it years later?

"Dad, what's that place up there?"
"Uh, that's the Hill of Foreskins."
"What happened up there?"
"Umm, I really don't want to talk about it . . . too painful."

Seriously, these men took a radical step of obedience to be identified as God's people in a painful and permanent way. Obviously, when God says "circumcise the sons of Israel a second time," he does not mean the men who had already been circumcised were to be circumcised a second time. By the way, the only two guys living who had gone through that ordeal already were Joshua and Caleb. That happened back in Egypt right before they were about to leave in the Exodus. In fact, Egyptians practiced circumcision as a religious ritual reserved for the priests and the upper class. So it would likely have been prohibited as a practice for the Israelites. But then on the eve of the Exodus, every male who ate the Passover in Egypt, native Israelite or stranger, was then circumcised (Exod. 12:43–49). And Exodus 12:50 tells us that at the command of God, "all the people of Israel did just as the LORD commanded Moses and Aaron." Fast-forward some forty years later, and God was requiring it of this new generation who came out of the wilderness and were poised to take the promised land.

But why the renewal of the rite of circumcision, and especially now? I mean, let's be real. Performing crude circumcision with stone knives on grown men would certainly leave the men of war vulnerable to attack because it totally incapacitated them for a while. In fact, a similar scenario actually played out in Genesis 34. The men of Shechem wanted to intermarry with the Hebrew women, so they agreed to be circumcised. Yet this was only subterfuge to render the Shechemites physically unable to defend themselves. The result? "On the third day, when they were sore, two of the sons of Jacob, Simeon and Levi, Dinah's brothers, took their swords and came against the city while it felt secure and killed all the males" (Gen. 34:25). Again, why circumcision now? It would render the men unable to fight. So why delay the attack on Jericho for this religious rite?

Verses 4–9 explain:

> And this is the reason why Joshua circumcised them: all the males of the people who came out of Egypt, all the men of war, had died in the wilderness on the way after they had come out of Egypt. Though all the people who came out had been circumcised, yet all the people who were born on the way in the wilderness after they had come out of Egypt had not been circumcised. For the people of Israel walked forty years in the wilderness until all the nation, the men of war who came out of Egypt, perished,

because they did not obey the voice of the LORD; the LORD swore to them that he would not let them see the land that the LORD had sworn to their fathers to give to us, a land flowing with milk and honey. So it was their children, whom he raised up in their place, that Joshua circumcised. For they were uncircumcised, because they had not been circumcised on the way. When the circumcising of the whole nation was finished, they remained in their places in the camp until they were healed. And the LORD said to Joshua, "Today I have rolled away the reproach of Egypt from you." And so the name of that place is called Gilgal to this day. (Josh 5:4–9)

First of all, circumcision was about establishing their identity as God's peculiar people. It was a permanent sign of the covenant promises of God to Abraham and to his descendants. It was therefore the means of becoming physically identified with the people of God for a male Israelite. Consequently, no uncircumcised male could legitimately partake of the Passover (Exod. 12:43–44). The Passover reminded them of God's deliverance of Israel from Egyptian bondage. Yet this deliverance had as its goal the possession of this land.

That leads to the second reason for this mass circumcision: none of the men born during their wilderness wanderings had been circumcised (Josh. 5:4–7). Lack of circumcision during those forty years was either further evidence of their faithless disobedience or, more likely, it was because they were unfit as a people under judgment to be circumcised. Remember, the sentence handed down by God in Numbers 14:26–35 was none of the men aged twenty and older would be allowed to enter the promised land (except for Joshua and Caleb), because they did not trust God to give them victory over the people of the land.

Instead, they had rebelled, and God judged them. Circumcision was a sign of God's covenant with Abraham and his descendants, which included the promised land as a possession (Gen. 17:8–9). Consequently, that rebellious generation under God's judgment could never possess the land, so that's why they were uncircumcised.

That brings us to the third reason: the new generation had to receive circumcision as a sign of the covenant before possessing the land God promised them. In fact, the Lord acknowledged the completion of circumcision with the words: "Today I have rolled away the reproach of Egypt from you" (Josh. 5:9). The Hebrew word used for "roll away" is from the same root for the place named "Gilgal," which means a circle, referring to the circle of stones placed at Gilgal when they were crossing the Jordan as a memorial of God's deliverance. The word for "wheel" comes from this word. So there is a play on words here for the sake of teaching an important truth.

Through the cutting away of the foreskin, circumcision symbolized the "rolling away" of the "reproach of Egypt." What was this disgrace? Naysaying Egyptians apparently mocked Israel for wandering aimlessly in the wilderness for forty years, concluding that Israel's God had abandoned them. Moses predicted Egypt would do this if God actually destroyed them out there in response to their faithless rebellion (Exod. 32:12; Num. 14:13–16; Deut. 9:28). This new generation was at the same moment of decision as the previous generation was in Numbers 14, poised to take the land. The rebellious generation disbelieved and disobeyed God and died in the wilderness. This new generation trusted and obeyed God and would possess the land. So circumcision was an act of consecration necessary before possessing the promised land.

Consequently, Gilgal, where they camped on the other side of the Jordan, now meant two things. First, it would stand for what God had done in miraculously rolling back the waters of the Jordan that they might cross on dry land. Second, it would remind Israel of their faithful obedience to God's law through the rite of circumcision, literally the "rolling away" of the foreskin. Thus, circumcision symbolized their consecrated commitment to God and his purposes as his people. It was the identifying mark that they belonged to him in covenant relationship.

Observing the Passover – Joshua 5:10

With circumcision accomplished, the people were spiritually ready and qualified to observe the Passover. It is also providential they crossed just in time to observe it on the fourteenth day of the month. God's timing is perfect. This was only the third Passover the people had kept. The first was in Egypt (Exod. 12:1–28), the second was at Mt. Sinai just before they broke camp to head toward the promised land (Num. 9:1–5), and the third time was here at Gilgal. Why the Passover? To relive their deliverance out of Egypt by the blood of the lamb sprinkled on the entries of their homes. But celebrating the Passover not only reminded them of their deliverance and redemption out of Egypt, but it looked forward to other victories, such as to the conquest of all the enemies entrenched in the promised land, and also to an ultimate victory over the enemy of our souls accomplished on Calvary. Passover naturally pointed to the cross where ". . . Christ, our Passover lamb, has been sacrificed" (1 Cor. 5:7).

Now that we are talking New Testament truths, circumcision has its parallel in baptism for the follower of Jesus. What a relief, right? I think I'll take dunking in water over cutting with knives, amen? But baptism pictures the death, burial, and resurrection of Christ. Obviously, the Passover has its New Testament parallel in the Lord's Supper or Communion. The Supper is the memorial meal where we are to remember the person and work of Christ, who was sacrificed as the Lamb of God who took our place and our punishment, bearing our sin that we might have life, abundant and eternal.

Baptism and communion or the Lord's Supper are referred to as ordinances of the church. They are required of those who identify as followers of Jesus Christ. The apostle Paul said of baptism:

> Do you not know that all of us who have been baptized into Christ Jesus were baptized into his death? We were buried therefore with him by baptism into death, in order that, just as Christ was raised from the dead by the glory of the Father, we too might walk in newness of life. For if we have been united with him in a death like his, we shall certainly be united with him in a resurrection like his. (Rom. 6:3–5)

Paul said of the Lord's Supper:

> For I received from the Lord what I also delivered to you, that the Lord Jesus on the night when he was betrayed took bread, and when he had given thanks, he broke it, and said, "This is my body, which is for you. Do this in remembrance of me." In the same way also he took the cup, after supper, saying, "This cup is the new covenant in my blood. Do this, as often as you drink it, in remembrance of me." For as often as you eat this bread and drink the cup, you proclaim the Lord's death until he comes. (1 Cor. 11:23–26).

As the rite of circumcision and Passover observance were to an Israelite, so baptism and the Lord's Supper are to a New Testament follower of Christ. Again, they identify us as belonging to Christ. As the leader in your home, you are to provide your family with a sense of identity. Obviously, when you get married, you will want to lead your wife in your identification with the Christian faith, specifically active membership in a local body of believers. If God blesses you with children, you will want to encourage them to identify as followers of Christ as well. There is nothing more fulfilling than helping your children understand and respond to the grace of God in the person of Jesus Christ, then see them baptized and take the Lord's Supper for the first time.

We identify with so many rival tribes today. It starts early with sports teams and schools, then it graduates to brands like Apple or Android, Coke or Pepsi, Ford or Chevy, Smith & Wesson or Sig Sauer, then eventually to political parties like Democrat or Republican. In fact, people sport a lot of different "team jerseys," finding their identity in their ethnic group, sexual preferences, economic philosophy, or whatever. Some are good, some neutral; others are harmful, even sinful. Yet the most important "jersey" of all is the one that identifies us as a follower of Jesus Christ. Do all you can to provide a sense of identity that is winsome and compelling so that the individuals God has placed in your charge get that one right. Praise God both my children did.

My (Cureton's) son, Will, received an education on identity one Saturday. He had only been married a few months when he came home to help old Dad deal with a big tree that had fallen on our property, perfect for restocking my rack of firewood. Having done the chainsaw work, we jumped in my truck and drove to an equipment rental business for a hydraulic log splitter. I didn't know the guy at the counter, but he matter-of-factly directed me to pick out a splitter and hook it up to my truck, and he would prep the paperwork. We did and I filled out my information on his rental form and produced my ID.

He took one look at my last name and asked: "Are you any relation to Pete Cureton?"

"Yes, that was my dad."

Everything changed from that moment. He lit up: "Hey, I worked with your dad out at the [BASF] plant. There was not a finer Christian man than Pete Cureton . . . ." After talking about my dad's godly qualities and untimely death, the guy said, "Let me see which one of those log splitters you picked. No, you need this other one; it's a better one. Man, it is so good to meet you and your son. I sure do miss your dad." We talked a few more minutes, then said our goodbyes.

Will and I headed out the door to my truck. He was pondering the whole transformation in that guy once he found out who we were related to, and I said, "Well, that was a lesson today about having a good name. The Bible says: 'A good name is to be chosen rather than great riches' (Prov. 22:1). You saw how much that means. I trust you will do the same with the Cureton name." Will nodded that he would, and he has! I couldn't be more proud of him as he carries not only the Cureton name, but more importantly, the name of Christ.

Providing a strong sense of identity is the foundation for a godly legacy. My dad did that for me. With God's help, I'm attempting to do that for my son. I feel confident he will do the same for his. So men, provide your family with an identity.

Pray

Father, we thank you for the high honor that is ours to be identified with your Son Jesus, who though fully God, was also the most godly man who ever walked this earth, taking our place and our punishment so that we could be called your sons and daughters by faith in him. God, help us to bear his name so winsomely and well that our wives, children, colleagues, and friends will want to identify with him by faith and obedience. And Lord, help us to leave a good name to our families. In Jesus's matchless name, Amen.

BATTLE BUDDY GROUP GUIDE

Week 2 – Man as a Provider

▶ The Provider Helping Others
LTG (RET.) Jerry Boykin from his book *Man to Man*

My father, Cecil Boykin, was a man who knew what was important in life. And as long as he lived, he remained true to his personal values.

When his mother and father were no longer able to manage the farm Cecil had grown up on, they were suddenly left with no place to live for their retirement. Although they had ten children, only one of them came up with a solution for their dilemma—that man was my father. Cecil was far from wealthy and didn't have the option of taking money out of a savings account or cashing in some Wall Street investments. Instead, he used his disability pension to provide for his parents by building a small home for them, because Cecil's family had always lived in rented homes.

A couple of years after Cecil's parents moved into the new home, his youngest sister, Faye, and her husband also moved in with their parents because Faye's husband was disabled and bed-ridden. After both my grandparents died, my father sold it to his nephew, Faye's son, who had also grown up there. Cecil sold the home for far less than what it was worth as a way of supporting his sister and her invalid husband.

I find myself at times wondering how many of today's generation would feel the way Cecil did or do what he'd done. I even wonder if I would have made that sacrifice in the same situation.

There's a biblical mandate for us, as fathers and sons, to take care of our families—including our extended families—and also to look after others as needs arise.

Cecil's habit of providing for others wasn't limited to his immediate family. One day he got word that his best friend had lost his home in a fire. At that time Cecil was struggling to pay his own bills.

But that didn't stop him: he cut corners and scraped together whatever he could. And he gave his friend all the cash he could find.

I remember that day—as he handed the cash to his friend—because it looked like so much money to me at the time. I would guess that it was no more than a hundred dollars in various denominations of bills, but to an eight-year-old it looked like a fortune. It left a powerful impression on me and just deepened my respect and admiration for him over the years.

Throughout my life my father exhibited many examples for me to follow concerning the responsibility a man has to care for those he loves and for those who are in need.

My father firmly believed that it wasn't the U.S. government's responsibility to take care of his parents, his children, his friends, or his neighbors. In fact, in his view, it was his role as an American who loved his country to help provide for others—as much as possible.

All Cecil Boykin ever wanted from his American homeland was opportunity. Everything else would come from his own hard work, self-reliance, and when necessary, generosity.[5] ◄

Group Debrief

In a society full of hurting and needy people, we often find many reasons not to help—whether it be our money, time, or other resources. While some of these reasons are valid, many become excuses that keep us from following God's command to help those in need. Consider the parable Jesus told in Matthew 25 about the great judgment coming when he will separate people like sheep and goats:

> "Then the righteous will answer him, 'Lord, when did we see you hungry and feed you, or thirsty and give you something to drink? When did we see you a stranger and take you in, or without clothes and clothe you? When did we see you sick, or in prison, and visit you?' "And the King will answer them,

'Truly I tell you, whatever you did for one of the least of these brothers and sisters of mine, you did for me.'" (Matt. 25:37–40 csb)

Recall the story you just read about Cecil Boykin. He could have allowed his own struggles to keep him from helping his friends and family, but instead he put his trust in the Lord by doing everything he could to provide for them even when it meant making difficult sacrifices.

Questions to Consider

- Can you think of any other biblical examples where men and women of God placed the needs of others above their own, even when they found themselves in difficult situations?

- What barriers might be keeping you from helping your friends, family, or those in need?

- What sacrifices can you make in order to help others?

- What are some things that might be holding you back from making those sacrifices? How can you surrender that to God?

CHAPTER 3
Man as an Instructor

In this chapter, we will explore the God-given role of instructor. When I say a man should be an instructor, I am not insinuating that you need to become an annoying know-it-all. You know the guy, the one who is always interrupting your conversations to brag about his expertise. Perhaps instead of instructor, you'd prefer to think of yourself as a teacher, a coach, or especially a mentor. Regardless, it is your responsibility to offer practical advice and wisdom, to inform and provide insight to your family and those you care about or influence, whenever and wherever you have the opportunity. To share timely information, seasoned wisdom, lessons learned, and a sense of history is vital to the next generation's development.

We should also offer insight and inspiration to other men within our circles of influence, so they can be better equipped to take their place as God's men in our churches, community, and this country. Nothing could be more important in this confused world than for more informed men to stand courageous for such a time as this, like the men of Issachar, who "had understanding of the times, to know what Israel ought to do" (1 Chron. 12:32). Consequently, serving others as a wise instructor is part of your responsibility as a man who leads.

Times to Teach – Joshua 4:1–24

Sitting around the kitchen table with my family after dinner, I (Cureton) unfolded what I believed to be God's next assignment for me individually and for us as a family. I took the time to revisit the "spiritual markers" in our lives where we had encountered God, particularly in providing direction. Then I proceeded to tell them God had once again provided clear guidance through specific verses of Scripture, through intense prayer and seeking to hear God's voice, through the circumstances that developed as a result, and through advice from others walking with God. My wife, Pat, joined me in explaining what this would mean for our family in general, and for Kristen and Will specifically. As you might expect, they had more questions than we had answers at the time. Yet before we were done, there was agreement on one thing, based on what God was evidently doing and saying: we were going to trust and obey God.

Moving your family to a new location for a new assignment can be a tough sell, especially when it means moving away from grandparents! What made it somewhat smoother for me in this instance were two factors: 1) As the instructor, I had already oriented my family to have a providential perspective of God's activity in our lives; and 2) I provided compelling evidence that God was central in this decision to move, reciting the key Scriptures God used to speak to me, recalling how he specifically answered prayer, rehearsing the numerous circumstances that lined up in that particular direction, and recollecting the wisdom from other godly people who simply helped clarify and confirm what God was doing. That experience became a "spiritual marker" we looked back on when things got tough. It was evidence the God who guides will also provide. Now, in case you are one of those who just doesn't quite understand this idea that God speaks to us, then let me assure you he does. It is rarely an audible voice, but he speaks through the Scriptures frequently when you are sincerely searching for an answer. Or he may even speak through dreams or with that still, small voice that is discussed in 1 Kings 19:11–13, when Elijah was seeking the Lord.

In Joshua 4, God instructed him to commemorate the awesome miracle of stopping the raging Jordan River. The priests carried the ark of the covenant ahead of the people, walked into the lapping waters of the rushing torrent, and the river literally fled from their feet. God miraculously rolled back the river so the whole nation could pass over on dry ground (chapter 3). The memorial was to be set up as a teaching tool to remind future generations to never fret over what is before us in the future when God is with us. The God who guides will also provide. And out of this encounter with Almighty God in Joshua 3–4 came several things worth remembering and passing on to the next generation.[1]

The People Were Sanctified

Look at 3:5: "Then Joshua said to the people, 'Consecrate yourselves, for tomorrow the LORD will do wonders among you.'" In the process of preparing to cross that river, there was a revival of sorts. They had gotten together and prayed, they had confessed sin, they asked for forgiveness and cleansing, and they had been sanctified and consecrated. They were spiritually prepared for what God wanted them to do next. Sometimes God brings us to a moment that is so vital, so critical, so important, that it calls for a new sense of holiness. Remember that. The people were sanctified.

Joshua Was Magnified

Look at 3:7: "The LORD said to Joshua, 'Today I will begin to exalt you in the sight of all Israel, that they may know that, as I was with Moses, so I will be with you.'" The KJV says: "This day will I begin to magnify thee in the sight of all Israel . . . ." Remember, Joshua was given the awesome assignment of being Moses's successor, and no doubt Joshua was a little intimidated by that, because God had to keep telling him in the first chapter: "Be strong and very courageous." And God told him: "Joshua, now that you're the leader, I'm going to do something so awesome through you that they will follow you like they followed Moses. I'm going to magnify you before the people." Did that happen? Look at 4:14, "On that day the LORD exalted Joshua in the sight of all Israel, and they stood in awe of him just as they had stood in awe of Moses, all the days of his life." So the people were sanctified and Joshua was magnified.

God Was Glorified

Note the response of the people to these developments:

> "So that all the peoples of the earth may know that the hand of the LORD is mighty, that you may fear the LORD your God forever." As soon as all the kings of the Amorites who were beyond the Jordan to the west, and all the kings of the Canaanites who were by the sea, heard that the LORD had dried up the waters of the Jordan for the people of Israel until they had crossed over, their hearts melted and there was no longer any spirit in them because of the people of Israel. (4:24–5:1)

Word got out about God delivering his people out of Egypt and bringing them to this land. Back in chapter 2, Rahab said, "The fear of you has fallen upon us, and that all the inhabitants of the land melt away before you. For we have heard how the LORD dried up the water of the Red Sea before you when you came out of Egypt, and what you did to the two kings of the Amorites" (2:9–10). Indeed, part of the purpose of Joshua setting up these memorials was so that "all the peoples of the earth may know that the hand of the Lord is mighty" (4:24). Something happened after these miraculous events in Joshua 3–4. News spread all over Canaan, and wherever people met they talked about the great God of Israel (cf. 5:1). So when the people crossed over, the people were sanctified, Joshua was magnified, and God was glorified. Remember that—God's miraculous deeds bring him glory.

The Word of God Was Verified

In the first part of chapter 3, God told Joshua, "This is what's going to happen, so tell the people to consecrate themselves and tell the priest to carry the ark of the covenant down into the waters of the Jordan; and when they do, you'll see the miracle." So the people of God took Joshua at his word because Joshua had taken God at his word. When you read chapter 3, you find out God did exactly what he told Joshua he was going to do. He stopped the raging river and the people crossed on dry ground. Consequently, God's word was verified. Remember that. God keeps his word. You see, Joshua was fulfilling his role as an instructor by teaching the Israelites to trust God. He believed God's promises and knew he had to instruct the people in the imperative to rely on God—not on men, or horses and chariots.

From Joshua 4, we learn God wants his people to always remember what he did for them on this day, so he asks Joshua to build a couple of memorials. That way these stacks of stones could be used as spiritual markers to help people recall how God miraculously enabled them to cross the Jordan River at flood stage. Joshua built one himself in the dry riverbed: "And Joshua set up twelve stones in the midst of the Jordan, in the place where the feet of the priests bearing the ark of the covenant had stood; and they are there to this day" (4:9). Picture how this played out.

The priests carried the ark of the covenant, which represented God's presence among his people, and marched out in front of the people, taking that gold-covered ark right into the edge of the raging river. And God rolled the river back when the feet of that first priest touched those waters, and then they walked out to the middle. What an unforgettable experience that must have been, not only to see those waters flee from under their feet, but to see that big mountain of water hovering, swirling, and pulsating above their heads, growing higher with every passing minute.

They had to stand there with that ark on their shoulders while all the children of Israel walked around them and then on to the other side! At any moment, if God released it, that mountain of water could have come crashing down and swept them all away. But those priests stayed right in the middle of that riverbed until the last Israelite had "clean passed over" (KJV). That is real faith! Sometimes God wants us to stand in the midst of a situation while a mountain of threatening circumstances builds higher and higher so we learn to trust him more deeply.

Some might ask: "What good is a monument in the middle of the Jordan after the waters returned and covered them?" Well, the river at this point was at flood stage, but it didn't stay that way. So when the waters of the Jordan receded during the late spring and summer, right at the spot where the people crossed over and where the priests had stood, this monument of stones appeared as a visible reminder that God had been faithful. God had providentially, supernaturally, and miraculously intervened.

Why Are Memorials Important?

All throughout Scripture, memorials remind us of experiences with God.

One of the first came after the flood. Once God had safely delivered Noah and his family, God put a memorial in the sky and said to Noah, "'Every time you see a rainbow, it is a memo-rial; it is a reminder of how I delivered you from the flood, and it is a promise that I'll never destroy the world with water'" (Gen. 9:12–17, paraphrase). So the rainbow is a memorial of God's faithfulness to Noah and his descendants.

Remember how God gave Abraham the sign of circumci-sion to separate the Hebrews from all the peoples around them. And God gave the Hebrews the Passover as a memorial meal to commemorate their deliverance from Egypt. Even the ark of the covenant and its contents served as a memorial. Do you remem-ber what was in it? Aaron's rod that budded, a golden urn filled with manna, and the two tablets of the Ten Commandments—all reminders of their sojourn in the wilderness and God's gra-cious provision. God loves memorials. In the previous chapter, we talked about the memorials given to us as Christians: bap-tism and the Lord's Supper.

Why did the Lord institute all these memorials, which were physical markers of God's providence? *Because we have a ten-dency to forget what God has done.* Moses wrote:

> "Take care lest you forget the LORD your God by not keeping his commandments and his rules and his statutes, which I command you today, lest, when you have eaten and are full and have built good houses and live in them, and when your herds and flocks multiply and your silver and gold is multiplied and all that you have is multiplied, then your heart be lifted up, and you forget the LORD your God, who brought you out of the land of Egypt, out of the house of slavery, who led you through the great and terrifying wilderness, with its fiery serpents and scorpions and thirsty ground where there was no water, who brought you water out of the flinty rock,

who fed you in the wilderness with manna that your
fathers did not know, that he might humble you and
test you, to do you good in the end. Beware lest you
say in your heart, 'My power and the might of my
hand have gotten me this wealth.' You shall remember the LORD your God, for it is he who gives you
power to get wealth, that he may confirm his covenant that he swore to your fathers, as it is this day."
(Deut. 8:11–18)

We have a tendency to forget God's deliverance when the
crisis is over or time has passed—that's why the Lord values
memorials to help us remember.

Memorials Encourage the Present Generation

Many times we think memorials are only for the future—
and they are—but they are also a powerful faith-building tool in
the present. Memorials encourage the present generation. Look
at Joshua 4:19–20, "The people came up out of the Jordan on the
tenth day of the first month, and they encamped at Gilgal on the
east border of Jericho. And those twelve stones, which they took
out of the Jordan, Joshua set up at Gilgal." Think about all of the
times the Israelites went into battle—there were certainly times
when they were discouraged from losing. But when they came
back to the camp at Gilgal, all they had to do was look over at
that stone monument Joshua had built to the glory of their great
God. That monument of stones from the midst of the Jordan
was a silent witness to the fact that their God had rolled back
the river so they could walk over on dry ground. No doubt they
came in and looked at that and said, "Man, what a mighty God
we serve!"

Memorials Educate the Next Generation

God wants us to use memorials as a teaching tool. Each of us men need to do our part in teaching the next generation about the memorials and even the monuments that reflect God's sovereignty, faithfulness, and omnipresence. Look at Joshua 4:6–7, then again in verses 21–23:

> "that this may be a sign among you. When your children ask in time to come, 'What do those stones mean to you?' then you shall tell them that the waters of the Jordan were cut off before the ark of the covenant of the Lord. When it passed over the Jordan, the waters of the Jordan were cut off. So these stones shall be to the people of Israel a memorial forever.... And he said to the people of Israel, 'When your children ask their fathers in times to come, What do these stones mean?' then you shall let your children know, 'Israel passed over this Jordan on dry ground.' For the Lord your God dried up the waters of the Jordan for you until you passed over, as the Lord your God did to the Red Sea, which he dried up for us until we passed over, so that all the peoples of the earth may know that the hand of the Lord is mighty, that you may fear the Lord your God forever."

Children need to be reminded of their spiritual heritage, and Joshua pictured a time when the children of the people who crossed over would come to their parents and say: "Hey, Mom and Dad, I was walking around in Gilgal and saw this big pile of stones. What do they mean?"

Joshua said, "Sit down with your kids and say: 'Let me tell you what those stones mean. You know there was a day when we were on the other side of the raging river Jordan and it was flooding its banks, and there was no way across. But kids, we trusted God, walked toward that river, and as soon as the priests stepped in, the river rolled back and we walked over on dry ground! Kids, that's the kind of mighty God we serve. He's your God!" Memorials educate the next generation.

Tony Perkins, President of Family Research Council, relates in our Stand Courageous conferences how he made this practical for his family:

> Just as Joshua puts up a stone monument as a testimony, we have what we call a Joshua basket. And it's filled with rocks. On each of those rocks we write a number. And in a journal that accompanies that basket of rocks there is a corresponding entry for each numbered rock. There we write about the faithfulness of God, of how he answered a prayer or how he saw us through a situation, something we were praying for. See, there's going to come a time when we're not here as parents, as fathers. But if the Lord takes me home tomorrow, I want my children to be able to go back to that basket, take out a rock, and read of God's faithfulness. I want my grandchildren and great grandchildren to read of his faithfulness in that journal. We need to be intentional about instructing our children about the greatness and glory of God.

Memorials Are Evidence to the Entire World

Memorials not only encourage the present generation and educate the next generation, they also provide evidence to the entire world concerning the true and living God (4:24). When the two spies went into Jericho, Rahab told them about their perspective of Israel's God. Look at Joshua 2:8–11:

> Before the men lay down, she came up to them on the roof and said to the men, "I know that the LORD has given you the land, and that the fear of you has fallen upon us, and that all the inhabitants of the land melt away before you. For we have heard how the LORD dried up the water of the Red Sea before you when you came out of Egypt, and what you did to the two kings of the Amorites who were beyond the Jordan, to Sihon and Og, whom you devoted to destruction. And as soon as we heard it, our hearts melted, and there was no spirit left in any man because of you, for the LORD your God, he is God in the heavens above and on the earth beneath."

Rahab said: "We saw what God did for you, and now we're convinced that your God is the true God of heaven and earth!" And God told Israel: "I want you to build these memorials in the midst of the river, and in the midst of the camp at Gilgal because I want the people of the nations to look at those stones and know that I am the true and living God." So God wants us to set up memorials to encourage the present generation, educate our children, and as evidence to a watching world that our God is the only true God.

Now, obviously God doesn't want us to necessarily stack stones everywhere we have an experience with him, but in our role as the instructor, he does want us to memorialize these encounters and relate them to our children and grandchildren, as well as to a watching world, that our God is the true and living God. With that in mind, here are three questions by way of application:

1. What is God doing in your life that should be memorialized? What has he done or what is he doing that should be passed on?

If you can't think of anything, then maybe you haven't encountered him lately, or maybe when you did, you shrank back from taking a step of faith. Yet if you will think about it, he's told you to get your feet wet, to trust him, to believe him, to march through the Jordan Rivers of life. Believe me, he'll be just as faithful to you as he was to those folks in the book of Joshua. When you see him solve an impossible situation and remove an insurmountable obstacle, you'll never forget it, and you'll want to create a memorial, a spiritual marker you can look back on and draw strength from; and it can be the same for those in your charge. What is God doing in your life that should be memorialized?

2. What legacy are you leaving to your children and grandchildren concerning God's wonderful works on your behalf? Are you rehearsing God's mighty acts with your children? Are you writing them down for the purpose of passing on your remembrances of your experiences with God? Have you told them how God provided? Write down an example.

I hope that when everything is said and done, my children will remember their dad was a man who walked with God, who experienced his presence and power, who saw God do mighty things. What kind of memorial are you leaving your children? What will they come to know about your God based on what you've experienced and passed on? What is God doing in your life that should be memorialized? What recorded spiritual legacy are you leaving your children?

3. What do your neighbors know about God from the memorials you have created? Can you think of something specific from your relationship with God you have been able to share with neighbors, colleagues, or acquaintances? Write down an example or at least write down something you could share when God provides an opportunity.

Again, one of the purposes of these memorials is to remind a watching world that we serve the true and living God. Can your unchurched neighbor see anything of the presence and power of God in your life? Has God made a visible, tangible difference in the way you think, speak, and act? Has he answered prayer in a way that speaks of his mighty power? What can your neighbors know about God from your encounters with him? When the world sees things happening through God's people that cannot be explained except that God himself has done them, then the world will be drawn to the God they see. Let your neighbors see miraculous signs of an all-powerful God, and like Rahab, they will declare that he is the one true God.

Pray

Father, thank you for the many memorials to your greatness that you give us along the way. May we set up "spiritual markers" in our lives and share them with our families. Father, we confess the reason why people are not attracted to the Christ we serve is because they can't see him at work in our lives. Lord, may the world see you at work in us so they will be drawn to you. In Jesus's name, Amen.

Learn to Discern – Joshua 2; 7; 9

As a leader, discernment is a valuable quality. To discern means to distinguish one thing from another, like true from false, good from bad, right from wrong. For a few, discernment is a spiritual gift (1 Cor. 12:10). For the rest of us, we have to learn it as a skill. Some of us learn it the hard way. Ever pulled the trigger on an online auction, thinking: *Man, what a deal!*—only to get it in the mail and toss it in the trash, thinking: *My dad always told me: "You get what you pay for"?* Or maybe in high school, your buddy talked you into a double date, setting you up with a girl you'd never met? Oh boy! Been there, done that, and I knew better. So you lost a few bucks or wasted an evening? No big deal, right? Yet as life progresses, the stakes can get higher, a lot higher. Your need for discernment to make sound decisions gets far more important, especially when you are married and have a family. There's a lot on the line when you make decisions.

Discernment is a vital skill in the Bible. Again, the sons of Issachar "had understanding of the times, to know what Israel ought to do" (1 Chron. 12:32). In the New Testament, Jesus chided the Pharisees because they lacked discernment. They could predict the weather because of the signs in the sky, but were unable to discern the signs of the times. Because they were more concerned about adding to the law, they were unable to discern God's truth and not only missed but murdered the Messiah (Matt. 16:1–3). Indeed, Hosea 4:14 says, "A people without understanding shall come to ruin." There are three keys to discernment in three stories from Joshua:

1. Investigate (chap. 2)
2. Interrogate (chap. 7)
3. Invocate or pray (chap. 9)

Investigate

In Joshua 2, the call is to investigate—spy out the land. Now this was nothing new for Joshua. Remember, he was a member of the original twelve-man recon unit that spied out the promised land back in the book of Numbers. God told Moses to choose a leader from each tribe for this purpose, and here were their instructions:

> "See what the land is, and whether the people who
> dwell in it are strong or weak, whether they are few
> or many, and whether the land that they dwell in is
> good or bad, and whether the cities that they dwell
> in are camps or strongholds, and whether the land is
> rich or poor, and whether there are trees in it or not.
> Be of good courage and bring some of the fruit of the
> land." (Num. 13:18–20a)

In a word, Moses told them to investigate and see what the
land is like. Now on the edge of the promised land forty years
later, Joshua resorted to sending out another recon team of two
for the same purpose—investigate. However, these spies were to
focus their attention on the great walled city of Jericho. So they
walked up the road leading to the city, slipped past the gates of
the city, and looked around at the fortifications and defenses; but
in the process they were found out and tried to flee. Providentially, they found refuge in a prostitute's house:

> And it was told to the king of Jericho, "Behold, men
> of Israel have come here tonight to search out the
> land." Then the king of Jericho sent to Rahab, saying,
> "Bring out the men who have come to you, who
> entered your house, for they have come to search out
> all the land." (Josh. 2:2–3)

When her house was searched, Rahab told a lie and sent
the soldiers off on a wild goose chase so the Hebrew spies could
escape. In return for her kindness, she and her household were
promised safety when Israel attacked. After Jericho fell, they
ended up becoming part of the people of Israel, and Rahab is
listed in the lineage of Jesus (Matt. 1:5).

The point is, the mission of the spies was to investigate. When you are trying to make a decision, one of the first things you will need to do is gather the facts. The original spies in Numbers 13 were to "see what the land is like," and the second group here in Joshua 2 was to "scout" the defenses of the city and the mood of the enemy. That involves intel gathering. Whether someone is buying a car, choosing a college, or settling on a career, we need to investigate. When there is a breakdown in a relationship or a moral failure in one of our children, we need to investigate. Proverbs 18:15 says, "An intelligent heart acquires knowledge, and the ear of the wise seeks knowledge." Investigation is the starting point on the road to discernment.

Interrogate

In Joshua 7, Joshua and the people of Israel experience their first defeat, and the task fell to Joshua to interrogate. You remember the story. After God miraculously brought down the walls of Jericho so Israel could win a great victory in chapter 6, the next town on the hit list was lowly Ai. As he did with Jericho, Joshua sent out a recon team to scout it out. They did their investigation. Yet instead of inquiring of the Lord, consecrating themselves, and seeking his battle plans like they did before Jericho, Joshua listened to his field generals who convinced him to send fewer troops into Ai. They had sized up the enemy and dismissed them as insignificant. "Don't tax the whole army with such a trivial task," they said. So Joshua only sent out a relative handful of troops, and they blundered into Ai and got whipped, because God was not with them. The reason? There was sin in the camp. Like Samson with his fresh buzz cut, the strength was not there, and Israel was embarrassed (Josh. 7:2–5).

Joshua is humbled and begins to inquire of God: "Why?" The answer: someone kept things from Jericho that were to be destroyed. In fact, we've already been told who the guilty party is in Joshua 7:1. Yet the Lord instructed Joshua to go through a series of lot-casting exercises to arrive at the answer (vv. 13–15). This no doubt served to escalate the anticipation and attention of the whole nation, which was compounded by the severe sentence: "And he who is taken with the devoted things shall be burned with fire, he and all that he has, because he has transgressed the covenant of the LORD, and because he has done an outrageous thing in Israel" (7:15). When Achan was fingered as the one responsible (v. 18), Joshua demanded: "My son, give glory to the LORD God of Israel and give praise to him. And tell me now what you have done; do not hide it from me" (v. 19).

Joshua confronted Achan and interrogated him. He needed to question him to get the truth, ask Achan to come clean. Of course, Achan immediately confessed the sin and spilled the beans, telling Joshua where the contraband was hidden in the ground beneath his tent. Then Joshua meted out the severe punishment God prescribed. They stoned Achan and his family then took him, his family, his animals, and his possessions and burned them to ash. Then they piled up more rocks on top of them as an "anti-memorial" and called that place the "Valley of Trouble" (vv. 20–26). I'll wager that spectacle cut down on anyone having "sticky fingers" for a while in Israel!

Allow me (Boykin) to share a personal story with you at this point. My personal ministry, Kingdom Warriors, was founded as I left the U.S. Army after thirty-six years of service. I set it up so I only saw the financial reports at the board meetings. I trusted the bookkeeper, so he had total control of, as well as access to, the ministry account. After ten years of ministry, I discovered almost by accident that the bookkeeper and the travel agent who arranged all travel were stealing from the ministry. In fact, they had taken tens of thousands of dollars over the years. As I investigated, I discovered that the travel agent was also a drug dealer, and the bookkeeper was a sexual deviant. I was really devastated by the whole thing because I had lacked discernment in the beginning to find reliable people for the ministry. One day I was praying about the situation, and, frankly, I fell into the self-pity trap as I prayed and tried to persuade God this was "just not fair." But as I poured out my heart to the Lord, he spoke to me through the Scripture in that still, small voice I hear so often. He simply said to me, "Get the sin out of your camp and I will bless your ministry."

I knew what I had to do. I dismissed both of them and filed charges against one of them. Since then, the ministry has seen the greatest abundance of resources and the most opportunities to minister to large numbers of people that we have ever had. Do you have sin in your camp you are blind to and unable to discern? Ask God to reveal it, and remove it immediately so your discernment may be restored just as mine was.

When faced with a decision and while trying to discern what to do, first investigate and then interrogate. For some decisions or situations, "interrogate" may be too strong a word, but you get the point. Ask questions. When you sense your child is struggling academically or with peer pressure or fill-in-the-blank, ask questions. When you are about to make a major purchase or change jobs or anything else that would make a huge impact on your family, ask questions. You can't come to a wise decision without investigation and interrogation—searching out the facts and asking probing questions. Thankfully, God graciously helped Joshua rectify the situation; they went on to victory over Ai, and God taught Joshua and the people of Israel a valuable lesson.

Invocate

The most important tool in discernment is prayer. In fact, it really isn't a step at all. Prayer should be our first response, not our last resort in decision making. The text that highlights this need comes next in Joshua 9. The word spread about another fallen city, and the fear of God fell over the people in that land. In 9:1–2 we find the various tribes of people decided to get together and form an alliance against Israel. So the Hittites, the Amorites, the Canaanites, the Perizzites, the Hivites, the Jebusites, the *Termites*—all the "-ites" you can think of—stopped fighting each other long enough to fight against Joshua!

Now about this same time, the Gibeonites, who were next on Joshua's hit list, had a better idea. They knew if they tried to surrender, they'd be slaughtered, and if they tried to fight, it would mean their funeral. They had a more subtle strategy. They figured, "Hey, if you can't beat 'em, join 'em." So the Gibeonites sent a delegation disguised as travelers from afar. They put on ragged clothes and worn-out sandals, and they loaded some donkeys with old wineskins and knapsacks filled with dry, stale bread. That's how the Gibeonites came straggling into Israel's camp, telling tall tales about coming from far away. "They acted deceptively," says verse 4 (csb), which is the same Hebrew word used of Satan in Genesis 3:1.

Joshua and the men of Israel bought their act hook, line, and sinker. Oh, they checked them out, they did investigate a bit. In fact, Joshua went so far as to interrogate a little in verse 8: "Who are you? And where do you come from?" These fakes and frauds lied through their teeth: "From a very distant country your servants have come, because of the name of the LORD your God." They pointed to their stale bread and cracked wineskins, their worn-out clothes and sandals, begging: "We are your servants. Come now, make a covenant with us" (vv. 9–11). While the Israelites inspected their knapsacks, maybe just a few more probing questions would have helped them make a better decision. Yet the biggest thing they failed to do was "invocate," that is, pray. Verse 14 says, "So the men took some of their provisions, but did not ask counsel from the LORD."

The slick Gibeonites sold their fake story, but Joshua and the leaders did not inquire of the Lord. They didn't seek God's counsel. They didn't pray! Consequently, they made a bad decision. They made a covenant, a peace treaty with the Gibeonites; the elders swore an oath to them, and then found out three days later the Gibeonites lied. Their town was only thirty miles away! Later, we will find out how much this bad decision cost Israel in terms of blood and treasure. Yet it could have been avoided if Joshua and Israel had simply prayed to God for wisdom.

As the instructor in the home, you not only need to investigate, interrogate, and invocate so you can discern the best way forward for your family, but you also need to impart the skill of discernment to them. Teach them how to do some old-fashioned homework and fact-finding; teach them the fine art o f asking some probing questions; but most of all, teach them how to seek God. How many bad decisions and awful disasters could be avoided if we would humbly pause and pray before we decide and act? Men, learn to discern and teach those in your charge how to do the same.

Pray

> *Father, we are grateful for those in the body whom you have given the spiritual gift of discernment. Yet most of us have not been given that gift, so we humbly ask as Solomon did for your wisdom. God, teach us to investigate and interrogate, but most of all to invocate, to seek your face, and ask for your counsel before we make decisions and act. We ask for your help to discern your will for us in every decision we face. In Jesus's name, Amen.*

Rehearse Your History – Joshua 24:1–13

My family knows it is coming. Sitting around the table at our home on Memorial Day, the Fourth of July, Thanksgiving, etc., I always have an informative activity for my immediate family, extended family, and invited guests. Typically, we circle up and pray, recognizing the significance of the day for us as Americans, and feast on the wonderful meal my wife and her partners in culinary crime have cooked up for us. Then before we take up our plates and the bodacious array of desserts arrives, we pause, and I will call everyone to attention and direct them to what I have prepared to commemorate that day.

For example, on Memorial Day, I had those present read excerpts of last letters home written by military personnel who made the ultimate sacrifice on the altar of freedom. On the Fourth of July, I had them read a brief bio of a signer of the Declaration that included some of the sacrifices they made. On Thanksgiving, we put out five kernels of Indian corn in a little netting sack tied with a ribbon at each place setting, then told how the Pilgrims nearly starved, getting down to a ration of five kernels of corn a day, relating how they prayed and God broke the severe drought with life-giving rain; and how they celebrated a bountiful harvest and Thanksgiving in 1623. These are some of the creative ways I try to rehearse our history as Americans, reminding them our national motto is, "In God We Trust."

We live in a generation that has lost touch with the past. Yes, we need to be a forward-looking people. Everyone knows you can't drive a car by staying glued to the rearview mirror. But every once in a while, it is good to glance in that mirror and see where we've been. To rehearse our history so we can remember who we are as a people. History is important, not simply because it demonstrates our ability to remember facts, but also because it gives us perspective for the present, and even helps us set our course into the future. We must know the sacrifices that have been made for this nation in order to be a proud American, especially at a time when so many citizens of this nation are being so critical of our homeland. They either do not know history or they are cherry-picking excerpts from it to suit their personal narrative.

In chapter 24:1–13, Joshua begins his final charge to the nation of Israel with a review. He traces God's hand of providence in the humble beginnings of the nation, and he takes them through nearly 600 years of history:

> Joshua gathered all the tribes of Israel to Shechem and summoned the elders, the heads, the judges, and the officers of Israel. And they presented themselves before God. And Joshua said to all the people, "Thus says the LORD, the God of Israel, 'Long ago, your fathers lived beyond the Euphrates, Terah, the father of Abraham and of Nahor; and they served other gods. Then I took your father Abraham from beyond the River and led him through all the land of Canaan, and made his offspring many. I gave him Isaac. And to Isaac I gave Jacob and Esau. And I gave Esau the hill country of Seir to possess, but Jacob and his children went down to Egypt. And I sent Moses and Aaron, and I plagued Egypt with what I did in the midst of it, and afterward I brought you out.
>
> "'Then I brought your fathers out of Egypt, and you came to the sea. And the Egyptians pursued your fathers with chariots and horsemen to the Red Sea. And when they cried to the LORD, he put darkness between you and the Egyptians and made the sea come upon them and cover them; and your eyes saw what I did in Egypt. And you lived in the wilderness

a long time. Then I brought you to the land of the Amorites, who lived on the other side of the Jordan. They fought with you, and I gave them into your hand, and you took possession of their land, and I destroyed them before you. Then Balak the son of Zippor, king of Moab, arose and fought against Israel. And he sent and invited Balaam the son of Beor to curse you, but I would not listen to Balaam. Indeed, he blessed you. So I delivered you out of his hand. And you went over the Jordan and came to Jericho, and the leaders of Jericho fought against you, and also the Amorites, the Perizzites, the Canaanites, the Hittites, the Girgashites, the Hivites, and the Jebusites. And I gave them into your hand. And I sent the hornet before you, which drove them out before you, the two kings of the Amorites; it was not by your sword or by your bow. I gave you a land on which you had not labored and cities that you had not built, and you dwell in them. You eat the fruit of vineyards and olive orchards that you did not plant." (24:1–13)

Notice in verse 4, Joshua's review of the history begins with God's call of Abraham out of idolatry. While Abraham had served other gods, God revealed himself to Abraham and called him out of Ur and brought him to Canaan, the land of promise. Though Abraham and his wife Sarah were long past child-bearing age and had no children, God miraculously gave them many descendants. Through Isaac and not Ishmael, and through Jacob and not Esau was the promise passed. Yet God providentially sent Jacob and his family down to Egypt.

By the time we get to verses 5–7a, a significant shift happens. All the third-person pronouns give way to first-person references. Here, the Lord refers to the present generation: "I brought you out." From now on it is primarily "you," not "they." Most of these Israelites had not been present at the Exodus, though some of them may have been children at the time. Only Caleb and Joshua remained who were adults at the time of the exodus.

In verses 7b–12, the forty years in the wilderness are summarized with two episodes, both of which came late in their wanderings. Here we read of the victories the Lord gave Israel over Sihon and Og, the Amorite kings whose kingdoms were east of the Jordan River. The other episode, recounted at length in the book of Numbers, related how the Lord thwarted the evil efforts of Balak, with the help of the prophet Balaam, to destroy the Israelites by divine curse, which God reversed. The short summary of Israel's history is concluded in verse 13 with a beautiful reminder that Yahweh had given the Canaanites into Israel's hands and had delivered the land he had long before promised to Abraham, the land flowing with milk and honey, the land with all its wealth, into Israel's possession.

An awareness of history was critical to the future of the Jewish people, and Joshua assumed the role of instructor. Joshua wanted to ensure that the current generation of Israelites was fully aware of their history and would be able to pass that on to their descendants. We should seek to do that as men.

Remembering this history is more than simply mental recall. To remember in the Bible is to participate. Interestingly, the apostle Paul gives us a similar perspective when he reminds a church full of Gentiles in Corinth that their forefathers were delivered from bondage in Egypt. This history is not simply the history of Israel from the fifteenth to the fourteenth centuries BC. It is our history—yours and mine. The exodus of Israel is a part of our history as believers, just as the cross is for us as Christians.

Our adoption into the biblical story is also true in a way for us as Americans. Have you ever considered that? The American story is *your* story. It is *our* story. And it is an amazing story.

America is the most prosperous, technologically advanced, compassionate, free nation on earth at this time in history. Consider the fact that America is the birthplace of inventions like the telegraph, telephone, lightbulb, airplane, internet, and GPS. Consider the fact that Americans represent only 4.4 percent of the world's population but command nearly 41.6 percent of the world's wealth.[2]

But America is not only a wealthy nation, we are a compassionate nation. We have freed more people from tyranny, helped more people rebuild from the ravages of war, delivered more humanitarian aid and disaster relief to those who are suffering than any other nation in the world. When people around the world are in trouble, to whom do they turn? They turn to us, the United States! We are not a perfect nation. We have dealt with some serious national sins (e.g., slavery) and still have our flaws, but America has been a force for good in the world, and America is still the wonder of the world. America is the greatest nation on the face of the earth! Consequently, as the instructors in our homes, we should instill a sense of patriotism and pride in America.

Yet many are losing pride in being American. Patriotism has plummeted since 9/11. A recent poll showed that only 50 percent of Americans ages 18–29 feel strongly patriotic and proud of their American heritage.[3] Why is that? I believe it is because they haven't learned our true history. They've been fed fake history by the liberal progressive "hate America" professors who populate most colleges and universities, most of which take federal dollars (translation: your tax money) to do so.

The narrative in most institutions of so-called "higher learning" is that America is led by and full of a bunch of greedy climate-destroying capitalists, who are racists, homophobes, transphobes, and bigots. The first explorers and settlers who came to America? They were white supremacist Europeans whose primary mission in America was to rape, pillage, pollute, and colonize, while executing Native Americans and enslaving Africans. Our Founding Fathers? They were a collection of rich, white slave-owning elites who got most of their ideas about government from French enlightenment atheists like Rousseau and Voltaire. While these men may have referenced "god" in the Declaration of Independence, they were mostly deistic rationalists whose god created the world but no longer intervenes in human affairs. Does any of this remotely resemble anything you were fed? If that's too extreme, perhaps you would agree that most of what passes as "American history" is presented in such a manner that in no way encourages students to be proud of our country. Consequently, it is not surprising that we are seeing polls reflecting that patriotism is at an all-time low.

How can we as instructors instill a proper perspective of America for those in our charge? Essentially, we need to help them recover the "lost episodes" from America's story, which help us understand what made America the greatest nation in the world. President Donald Trump made famous the campaign phrase, "Make America Great Again." What we need to know is what made America great to begin with. I would argue that America is great because, for the most part, those who immigrated and settled here, those who founded and fought for our nation, those who drafted our Declaration of Independence and crafted our Constitution, honored the God of the Bible.

The Pilgrims

The first permanent settlement in what became the thirteen original colonies of America was in Jamestown, Virginia, in 1607. The primary driver behind it was Rev. Richard Hakluyt, who presented his case to Queen Elizabeth I back in 1584: "Wee shall by plantinge there inlarge the glory of the gospell, and from England plante sincere relligion, and provide a safe and a sure place to receave people from all partes of the worlds that are forced to flee for the truthe of God's worde."⁴ Hakluyt was the first to proclaim the providential purposes of America as a haven for the persecuted and a launch pad for gospel missions. When King James I issued the charter for the Virginia colony, it contained this missionary motive of "propagating of Christian Religion to such People, as yet live in Darkness . . . ."⁵ In fact, true to Hakluyt's vision, America sends more missionaries and more money for mission endeavors than any other nation in the world. When the first settlers landed on April 26, 1607, the Rev. Robert Hunt had prayer and later erected a cross at the spot. In the Jamestown Church in 1614, Pocahontas was baptized into the Christian faith, changing her name to Rebecca, because she identified with the story in Genesis 25; then she was married in that church to John Rolf.⁶ Also in the Jamestown Church, the first elected representative government in America met on July 30, 1619.⁷

The Pilgrims followed in late 1620, signing the Mayflower Compact before they left the ship to establish the colony. It begins: "In the name of God . . . ," and states their reason for coming: "For the glory of God and the advancement of the Christian faith . . . ."⁸ When they disembarked, chronicler William Bradford reports: "Being thus arrived in a good harbor and brought safe to land, they fell upon their knees & blessed ye God of heaven who had brought them over ye vast & furious ocean, and delivered them. . . . What could now sustain them but the Spirit of God and His grace?"⁹ Once established on the land, they repaid the Native Americans for the caches of corn they found and made a mutual defense treaty with several tribes that lasted over fifty years. Plus, both Jamestown and Plymouth were established under a mandated socialist system—which almost proved fatal—but both settlements ditched this system in favor of private property ownership and a capitalist system. The result was productivity and plenty.¹⁰

The Puritans who followed them in 1630 sought to establish a "Shining City on a Hill."[11] They quickly started schools and a college named after the Rev. John Harvard in 1636. They emphasized rigorous study of God's Word, inquiry into the sciences, and pursuit into all fields of knowledge as a part of discovering more of God's glory. In 1643, the New England colonies formed a covenant, and in it they too gave the same reason for their coming to America: "Whereas we all came into these parts of America with one and the same end and aim, namely, to advance the Kingdom of our Lord Jesus Christ and to enjoy the liberties of the Gospel . . . ."[12]

In 1639, these Puritans created the first Constitution in America, the Fundamental Orders of Connecticut (the Constitution State),[13] and it was based on Rev. Thomas Hooker's sermon out of Deuteronomy 1:13: "Choose for your tribes wise, understanding, and experienced men, and I will appoint them as your heads." Again, our representative form of government dates back to Jamestown, Plymouth, and the Bay Colonies, and in every charter, covenant, and constitution, there was an acknowledgment by the colonists of their dependence upon Almighty God. Additionally, the famed "Protestant work ethic" brought here by the Pilgrims and the Puritans who followed them emphasized hard work, discipline, and frugality as a part of their Christian values.[14] They laid the foundation for the greatest wealth-generating nation in world history.

The colonial acknowledgment of God continued during the War of Independence from Great Britain. The Declaration of Independence is truly a "declaration of dependence" upon Almighty God, as it refers to God four times in the text:

- "The Laws of Nature and of Nature's God . . ."
- "All Men are created equal, they are endowed by their Creator with certain unalienable Rights . . . ."

- "Appealing to the Supreme Judge of the World for the Rectitude of our Intentions . . ."
- "With a firm Reliance on the Protection of divine Providence . . ."

The Founding Fathers

The Second Continental Congress and their successors voted to have paid chaplains, recommended a version of the Bible to the American people, and made no less than fifteen proclamations calling for prayer for thanksgiving or prayer for repentance and fasting during the eight-year war.[15] Certainly, the war effort was the subject of much prayer. In fact, a special Congressional Prayer Room was added to the Capitol in 1954 with a kneeling bench, an altar, an open Bible, and the words of Psalm 16:1 in an inspiring stained-glass depicting Gen. George Washington kneeling in prayer.[16] At the end of the war in June 1783, Washington wrote the governors of the thirteen colonies, relating his prayer for them:

> I now make it my earnest prayer, that God would have you, and the State over which you preside, in his holy protection; that he would incline the hearts of the citizens to cultivate a spirit of subordination and obedience to government [Rom. 13:1]; to entertain a brotherly affection and love for one another [Rom. 12:10] . . . and finally, that he would most graciously be pleased to dispose us all to do justice, to love mercy [Micah 4:6], and to demean ourselves with that charity, humility, and pacific temper of mind, which were the characteristics of the Divine Author of our blessed religion [Heb. 12:2], and without humble imitation of whose example in these things, we can never hope to be a happy nation.[17]

Washington encouraged obedience to Scripture by urging Americans to submit to governing authority, love one another, do justice, love mercy, and to imitate the love and humility of Christ. The Treaty of Paris to end the war begins: "In the Name of the Holy & undivided Trinity . . . ."[18]

During the Constitutional Convention in 1787, the venerable elder statesman Ben Franklin called on members deadlocked in debate to pray. James Madison records his impassioned plea:

> Mr. President . . . [H]ow has it happened, Sir, that we have not hitherto once thought of humbly applying to the Father of Lights [James 1:17] to illuminate our understanding? In the beginning of the Contest with Great Britain, when we were sensible of danger, we had daily prayer in this room for Divine protection. Our prayers, Sir, were heard, & they were graciously answered. All of us who were engaged in the struggle must have observed frequent instances of a superintending Providence in our favor.
>
> To that kind Providence we owe this happy opportunity of consulting in peace on the means of establishing our future national felicity. And have we now forgotten that powerful Friend? Or do we imagine we no longer need His assistance? I have lived, Sir, a long time, and the longer I live, the more convincing proofs I see of this truth that God Governs in the affairs of men [Dan. 4:17; 2 Chron. 20:6]. And if a sparrow cannot fall to the ground without His notice [Matt. 10:29], is it probable that an empire can rise without His aid [Dan. 2:21]?
>
> We have been assured, Sir, in the Sacred Writings, that "except the Lord build the House, they

labor in vain that build it" [Psalm 127:1a]. I firmly
believe this; and I also believe that without his con-
curring aid we shall succeed in this political building
no better than the Builders of Babel [Gen. 11:1–9].
We shall be divided by our partial local interests; our
projects will be confounded, and we ourselves shall
become a reproach and bye word down to future ages
[Deut. 28:37].

And what is worse, mankind may hereafter
from this unfortunate instance, despair of establishing Governments by Human wisdom and leave it to
chance, war and conquest.

I therefore beg leave to move that henceforth
prayers imploring the assistance of Heaven [Neh. 2:4],
and its blessing on our deliberations, be held in this
Assembly every morning before we proceed to business, and that one or more of the clergy of this city be
requested to officiate in that service.[19]

Ben Franklin's call for prayer seemed to quell some of the
dissension, prompted a recess to meet in a church to celebrate
independence, and eventually the majority affirmed the new
Constitution. Ultimately, Franklin's plea led to the practice of
daily prayer before every session of Congress. His speech pow-
erfully affirms our motto, "In God We Trust."

In the War of 1812, our second war for independence
with Great Britain, the Capitol building and the White House
in Washington, D.C., were burned, and the future of America
looked grim. After God intervened to expel the British from our
capital with a storm of biblical proportions, Fort McHenry and
Baltimore providentially withstood an all-out onslaught by the
British. In light of those events, Francis Scott Key, inspired by

seeing the defiant flag over the fort, penned a poem on September 14, 1814, titled "Defence of Fort McHenry." It became our National Anthem, "The Star-Spangled Banner," and its fourth verse reads like a prayer:

> . . . Blest with vict'ry and peace may the heav'n rescued land
> Praise the power that hath made and preserv'd us a nation!
> Then conquer we must, when our cause it is just,
> And this be our motto—"In God is our trust." . . .[20]

The Civil War, World War I, and World War II

In the Civil War, where brother fought against brother, we cleansed the land of the national sin of slavery. It came at the cost of nearly 650,000 lives. Republican President Abraham Lincoln's Second Inaugural Address (only 703 words long), given a little over a month before his assassination, is one of the most important theological documents written by any American president. Specifically, Lincoln reflects on God's sovereign purposes in the Civil War and their role in bringing the country back together. He cites the irony that, "Both read the same Bible and pray to the same God, and each invoke His aid against the other." In the process, Lincoln mentions God fourteen times and quotes the Bible at least three times. Reaching a climax, Lincoln declared:

> Fondly do we hope—fervently do we pray—that this mighty scourge of war may speedily pass away. Yet, if God wills that it continue, until all the wealth piled by the bond-man's two hundred and fifty years of unrequited toil shall be sunk, and until every drop of blood drawn with the lash, shall be paid by another drawn with the sword, as was said three thousand years ago, so still it must be said "the judgments of the Lord are true, and righteous altogether" (Psalm 19:9).[21]

In the first World War, Private Alvin C. York was conflicted about entering the Army because of his personal beliefs as a devout Christian, but God gave him assurance that he would return home safely. In the midst of the Battle of Argonne, York faced overwhelming odds: "The bullets went over my head and on either side. But they never touched me [Psalm 91:7–8]. . . . So I am a witness to the fact that God did help me out of that hard battle; for the bushes were shot up all around me and I never got a scratch." York led an attack on an enemy machine gun nest, single-handedly killing at least twenty-three German soldiers, three of whom were officers, and capturing an astounding 132 men. For his bravery, Alvin York was made a sergeant and received the Medal of Honor. The hero of WWI declared: "God will be with you if you will only trust Him."[22]

In World War II, American forces liberated two continents and rescued untold millions from the tyranny of Nazi Germany and Imperial Japan. Democratic President Franklin Delano Roosevelt rallied the nation with a six-minute prayer over the radio on the evening of D-Day.[23] He called our mission a "Great Crusade." Shops closed and churches opened for prayer. General Eisenhower concluded his D-Day orders by calling on the men to "beseech the blessing of Almighty God upon this great and noble undertaking."[24] The collective prayers of the American people were answered, and victory came first in Europe and then in Asia a little over a year later. Our continued trust in God made the difference.

We could go on and on about the faith and heroism displayed in Korea, Vietnam, Iraq, Afghanistan, and other places around the world, as well as right here at home during 9/11. But those are just a few brief stories, some lost episodes from our rich Christian history and heritage. It falls on us to take up the torch of liberty and carry it forward. The sacrifices made by so many Americans to preserve freedom for ourselves and for other people around the globe should give every American a right to feel patriotic and proud. Consequently, every man should seek to instill some of that pride in the hearts of his family members and those in his charge.

Do you feel ill-equipped to instruct your family about America's Christian heritage? You are not alone. Here are a couple of books that may give you a broad chronological sweep: Benjamin Hart's *Faith and Freedom: The Christian Roots of American Liberty* is very readable but unfortunately contains no footnotes, only a solid bibliography. The other resource is a two-for-one: *The Founder's Bible* with stories from American history by Christian historian David Barton, which gives you the benefit of reading a Bible that has great history stories sprinkled in its pages.

When we remember what God has done in the past, it creates a solid foundation for our perspective on the events of the present. Joshua 24 teaches us that the memories of the past and our hopes of the future help us understand how we are to live right now. That's why rehearsing our history is so vitally important for every man to do in his role as the instructor. Psalm 78:3–4 clearly lays out our task as instructors:

> Things that we have heard and known, that our fathers have told us. We will not hide them from their children, but tell to the coming generation the glorious deeds of the LORD, and his might, and the wonders that he has done.

Pray

God of Abraham, Isaac, and Jacob, we praise you that you are our God as well. We are thankful we are also a part of this great and glorious story, that Israel's history has become our history by virtue of our faith in Jesus Christ. And Lord, thank you for America. It has been sown with the seeds of the gospel, watered by the blood of patriots, and cultivated by the hand of your providence. May we faithfully pass the stories of your praiseworthy acts, your might, and your wondrous works to the next generation. In Jesus's name, Amen.

BATTLE BUDDY GROUP GUIDE

Week 3 – Man as Instructor

▶ The Instructor Motivates with Shared Heritage
LTG (RET.) Jerry Boykin from his book *Man to Man*

When I was a young lieutenant, the U.S. Army founded what has become one of the most famous and renowned organizations in the military today: the U.S. Army Ranger Battalions. Up until then, there had been some small Ranger units in Vietnam, but this was going to be a contemporary, modern, post-Vietnam Ranger battalion.

U.S. Army Chief of Staff General Creighton W. Abrams ordered the activation of the first Ranger battalion in 1973 at Fort Stewart, Georgia. I was blessed to be a part of it. We would fall out in formation on the parade grounds at Fort Stewart, and the commander of that unit, Lieutenant Colonel Kenneth Leuer, would stand on an elevated platform before we did our morning exercise, and he would recite the history from where we derived our lineage. And he would say, "Gentlemen, we are descendants of Merrill's Marauders. The Marauders' motto was *sua sponte*, 'of my own accord.' It could be translated as, 'This I freely give.'"

Merrill's Marauders were in the jungles of Burma for ten months, fighting behind Japanese lines to open a road through the jungle to China. They were there to deliver aid to Gen. Chiang Kai-shek's Nationalist Army, which was locked in a stalemate with the Imperial Japanese Army. They went into that jungle with three thousand men, and they came out ten months later with three hundred. Of their own accord, they sacrificed themselves.

I was not the only young officer who began to take pride in our forebears and their exploits. Everybody out there on that field realized the fact that we were the descendants—we were the next generation—of these great men that had done incredible things. And we all wanted to be just like them, to do anything we could to preserve their memory and to live up to their legacy because we were the descendants of Merrill's Marauders. . . .

We would recite the Ranger Creed every morning. The Battalion commander was making the point that history was just as important as physical training. Only after he gave us the history did our physical training begin. And sometimes it was brutal.

LTC Leuer realized how important it was for us to understand the proud tradition of this unit now being formed. He believed it was important for us to know the history of our forebears, of those who went before us. Look today at the incredible combat record of the Rangers and how they have fought against incredible odds— they've fought sacrificially, and they also had a very high casualty rate. But their history has been carried on and passed down from generation to generation to those who followed us after we created the first Ranger Battalion.

Why did that history help us as young warriors to fulfill our military assignments with dedication, determination, and courage? Because our commander was making us more than aware that we were walking in the footsteps of fabled American heroes, and we were meant to live up to their example. He wanted us to realize their history would soon be our history.[25] ◀

Group Debrief

Knowing our history is vital to our future. While it is important to learn from the success of our ancestors, we must also learn and turn away from their mistakes. Like Merrill's Marauders, some leave behind a legacy we should be encouraged to follow. However, others leave behind a legacy their descendants wouldn't be proud of. Even if the latter is the case, we should heed the words of Joshua 24:2, 14:

> Joshua said to all the people, "This is what the LORD, the God of Israel, says: 'Long ago your ancestors, including Terah, the father of Abraham and Nahor,

lived beyond the Euphrates River and worshiped other gods. . . . Therefore, fear the LORD and worship him in sincerity and truth. Get rid of the gods your fathers worshiped beyond the Euphrates River and in Egypt, and worship the LORD." (Josh. 24:2, 14 CSB)

Questions to Consider

- What lessons in American history do you think are important to teach your children? Which lessons should we be encouraged by, and which ones should we look at as cautionary tales?

- What about your family history? What does your family legacy look like? Is it something you are proud of? If not, how can you turn it around?

- Good or bad, what do you want your children and future generations to learn from your history? How can you use your family history to encourage your children to live a God-honoring life?

- How can you make sure to build a legacy that will give your children and their children a history to be proud of?

CHAPTER 4

Man as a Defender

In this chapter, we will explore the God-given role of defender. Remember, Genesis 2 gives us a picture of God delegating authority to the man. Specifically, "The LORD God took the man and put him in the garden of Eden to work it and keep it" (Gen. 2:15). It was not only Adam's purpose to work, but also to watch. Again, the Hebrew word translated "watch" means to keep, guard, protect, or have charge of. Every man is given a certain domain—his garden, if you will—to protect from threat. This points to Adam's leadership role as the defender of the garden, and later, his wife and family. Consequently, defender is one of the major roles and responsibilities God has delegated to us as men.

Fight for Your Family – Joshua 6; 8

It is 1:30 a.m. at a home in the cul-de-sac of a normally peaceful neighborhood. There is a knock at the door. The man of the house answers. It is a young woman who claims she is having car trouble. The man of the house is suspicious. He excuses himself and grabs the most accessible weapon: the little .22-caliber pistol he just bought his wife as a gift for Mother's Day. When he returns and begins to open the door, two heavily armed men try to push the door open and begin shooting, firing multiple rounds into the house. Instinctively, the man of the house takes a defensive position and begins returning fire, blindly shooting but killing one of the three intruders and wounding another.

The surviving suspects were apprehended and brought to justice. Sheriff Esco Jarnagin says of Scott Knight: "He was very brave in doing that—defending his home and family—because if he had not taken the action he took, I'm certain we would have some homicides of innocent people."[1] Jarnagin said with all the shots fired, the Knight family "amazingly" escaped any injuries. In my estimation, Scott Knight is a hero. He did exactly what every man, every husband, every father ought to do when faced with a situation like that. He successfully defended himself, his family, and his property using a gun.

As you read that true story, maybe you started thinking: *What would I do in a situation like that? How would I deal with it?* Well, if you're like me, you'll make sure you have a weapon and know how to use it. Better yet, you'll have multiple weapons, and everyone in your family will know how to operate them. Today, you can't afford not to be armed and have a plan to defend yourself, your family, and your property. But let's not miss the point of this story and today's study by simply discussing the exercise of our Second Amendment right to bear arms. The point is, men are to be defenders and protectors of those entrusted to their care. If you are a husband, that means your wife. If you are a father, that includes your children.

To state it plainly: as a man, you are responsible for the physical security of your family. God has designed the sexes in such a way that men typically possess greater physical strength than women. Plus, God has wired men in such a way that we feel a need or desire to be defenders. Consequently, you are to use this God-given strength to protect your wife and ensure that she feels secure, which is a basic need felt by every woman. She needs to know you will protect her even at the cost of your own life. Your children need to know they can count on Dad to protect them against threats. Pastor John Piper expresses this responsibility vividly:

> If there is a sound downstairs during the night and it might be a burglar, you don't say to her: "This is an egalitarian marriage, so it's your turn to go check it out. I went last time." And I mean that even if your wife has a black belt in karate. After you've tried, she may finish off the burglar with one good kick to the solar plexus. But you better be unconscious on the floor, or you're no man. That's written on your soul, brother, by God Almighty. Big or little, strong or weak, night or day, you go up against the enemy first. Woe to the husband—and woe to the nation—that send their women to fight their battles.[2]

Exodus 22:2 says, "If a thief is found breaking in and is struck so that he dies, there shall be no bloodguilt for him." Bottom line: you have the right to protect your home, your family, and your property. That verse is the basis for what we call the "Castle Doctrine." That is, a man's home is his "castle," and he is the defender and protector of his castle and all within it. Founder James Wilson, signer of the Declaration and Constitution and U.S. Supreme Court Justice, declared: "[E]very man's house is deemed, by the law, to be his castle; and the law, while it invests him with the power, enjoins on him the duty, of the commanding officer."[3]

Nehemiah mobilized the people of Israel to rebuild the walls around Jerusalem and encountered opposition, telling us that they not only prayed, but set a guard day and night because of the threat (4:9). Further, Nehemiah strategically positioned them to defend against attack: "So in the lowest parts of the space behind the wall, in open places, I stationed the people by their clans, with their swords, their spears, and their bows" (4:13). Then Nehemiah rallied the people: "Do not be afraid of them. Remember the Lord, who is great and awesome, and fight for your brothers, your sons, your daughters, your wives, and your homes" (v. 14b). Nehemiah apparently had them build with a trowel in one hand and ready for battle with a sword in the other hand (vv. 17–18). Again, the principal object of being armed with weapons was the defense of their families as well as their fellow Israelites. That same responsibility falls primarily to us men.

Looking at the biblical text in the book of Joshua, it is clear the men took their role as defenders and protectors seriously. There is a lot of fighting going on. When God miraculously brought down the walls of Jericho, Joshua 6:20–21 reports: "The people went up into the city, every man straight before him, and they captured the city. Then they devoted all the city to destruction . . . ." After experiencing defeat in Ai and dealing with the sin in the camp, God assured Joshua of victory in their second battle (8:18–19): "Then the LORD said to Joshua, 'Stretch out the javelin that is in your hand toward Ai, for I will give it into your hand.' And Joshua stretched out the javelin that was in his hand toward the city. And the men in the ambush rose quickly out of their place, and as soon as he had stretched out his hand, they ran and entered the city and captured it. And they hurried to set the city on fire." There is an old saying that bears repeating here: "The true soldier fights not because he hates what is in front of him, but because he loves what is behind him."

Think about that last phrase. How does this apply in your own life when it comes to motivation as a defender?

Perhaps there is a thoughtful brother who is uncomfortable with the brutality in all this Old Testament war and bloodshed, and he raises the question: *Didn't Jesus say we are to love our enemies?* Yes, he did (Matt. 5:44; Luke 6:27). But that was not a word to a nation; that is a word for you as an individual. Look at the context and it is clear. As a follower of Christ, when an individual opposes us, particularly because of our faith in Christ, we are to love that person. That doesn't mean we run up and give them a big hug every time we see them. The love Jesus speaks of is not touchy-feely emotional, but it is intensely practical. In Luke 6:27–28, Jesus says, "Love your enemies, do good to those who hate you, bless those who curse you, pray for those who abuse you." That's how we are to love our enemies, seeking their highest good. But again, this has nothing to do with a nation faced with an armed force in the context of war.

Someone might say, "Fair enough, but I object to war as well." OK, it is not my purpose to present a full biblical defense of war, let alone unpack Augustine's just war theory.[4] So here's the brief answer. Because of Adam and Eve's sin, we live in a sinful and broken world. By nature, God is holy and must punish sin. Yet God "is not slow to fulfill his promise as some count slowness, but is patient toward you, not wishing that any should perish, but that all should reach repentance" (2 Pet. 3:9). Since not all do come to repentance, judgment is necessary. God uses various means to mete out his justice, one of the most extreme of which is war. Sometimes he used his people to punish nations who were evil. Sometimes he used evil nations to punish his own sinful people.

What we are reading about in the pages of Joshua is primarily the former case. In fact, God predicted to Abram (a.k.a. Abraham) all the way back in Genesis 15 that Israel would go into bondage in a foreign land (Egypt) for 400 years, then return to the land of Canaan to reclaim it, even giving the reason behind his timing: "And they shall come back here in the fourth generation, for the iniquity of the Amorites is not yet complete" (v. 16). These evil people who inhabited the land of promise during

Israel's slavery in Egypt and wanderings in the wilderness were given opportunity to repent, did not, and all that was left was God's judgment meted out through Joshua and his army. In fact, God told Joshua to kill them all once he crossed the Jordan River, speaking of the inhabitants of the promised land.

Satisfied? If not, we hate to break it to you, but this current age is going to end with a war to end all wars. The same Jesus who was born as a babe in Bethlehem, blessed the little children, wept over the city of Jerusalem, and willingly laid down his life as a sacrifice on that cross, is the same Jesus who is coming again. But his Second Coming will be completely different. When he comes again, our Lord is going to return on a white horse with his white robe soaked in blood, wielding a two-edged sword to make war on the forces of evil. You can read all about it in Revelation 19:11–21. War is a part of God's purposes and plans to punish and defeat evil, and yet every human life is the object of his care and concern. God told the prophet Ezekiel: "Say to them, As I live, declares the Lord GOD, I have no pleasure in the death of the wicked, but that the wicked turn from his way and live; turn back, turn back from your evil ways, for why will you die, O house of Israel?" (Ezek. 33:11).

Again, we can hear that thoughtful brother asking: "Didn't Jesus say in the Sermon on the Mount: 'Blessed are the Peace-makers'" (Matt. 5:9)? He did. Paul also said, "If possible, so far as it depends on you, live peaceably with all" (Rom. 12:18). Sometimes it is not possible to make peace with people, especially if they are attacking a family member with intent to do bodily harm. What about: "Do not resist the one who is evil. But if anyone slaps you on the right cheek, turn to him the other also" (Matt. 5:39)? Jesus is making a reference to a Semitic form of insult, a back-handed slap, not a threat to do bodily harm. When threatened with bodily harm, David evaded King Saul's spear, Jesus escaped an angry mob threatening to throw him off a cliff, Paul eluded King Aretas in Damascus in a basket over the wall. "Turning the other cheek" does not mean handing the spear back to demon-possessed King Saul and saying: "Sorry you missed me. Go ahead and take another shot." Obviously, sometimes evading an attack is not possible. Sometimes you have to stand your ground to protect and defend. For that you need a weapon.

In fact, Jesus told his disciples to buy a weapon. Check it out in Luke 22:36–38: "But now let the one who has a moneybag take it, and likewise a knapsack. And let the one who has no sword sell his cloak and buy one. For I tell you that this Scripture must be fulfilled in me: 'And he was numbered with the transgressors' [Isa. 53:12]. For what is written about me has its fulfillment.' And they said, 'Look, Lord, here are two swords.' And he said to them, 'It is enough.'" On the eve of his death, the Lord Jesus basically told his disciples: "Men, change of plans. Remember when I sent you out before, I told you not to worry about taking all that stuff with you [see Luke 10:1-6]? Well, I'm going to the cross, rising from the tomb, then ascending to the right hand of the Father. But after I'm gone, you are going to need your money and your weapons. And if you don't have a weapon, go buy one." Jesus is telling his disciples to possess weapons, presumably with a view to use them in defense of themselves and their families. This was not meant to be an exhortation to build his church with the sword as is the case with Islam; rather, it was a warning in building the church, they would be challenged by those who would try to stop them in their quest to fulfill the task that God was assigning them.

We know what that thoughtful brother is about to bring up next. There's another saying of Jesus about people taking up arms some say argues the contrary. In Matthew 26, when Peter used his sword to cut off the ear of a servant of the Jewish high priest, Jesus responded: "Put your sword back into its place. For all who take the sword will perish by the sword. Do you think that I cannot appeal to my Father, and he will at once send me more than twelve legions of angels? But how then should the Scriptures be fulfilled, that it must be so?" (vv. 52–54).

Read those verses in context, and they still support the position of possessing weapons for defense. First, Jesus did not want his disciples to stand in the way of his crucifixion or start a military uprising against Rome. If Peter took up the sword, he would be opposing God's sovereign plan for the cross and signing his own death warrant: "For all who take the sword will perish by the sword." Jesus was saying: "Peter, I'm going to the cross; this is God's plan, so let it happen without a fight." Second, by implication, we can't advance the kingdom of God by force of arms. Third, in the very same verse, Jesus told Peter to put his sword "in its place," at his side. He didn't say "give it away" or "throw it away." The Lord Jesus said: "Keep it. Put it in its place." Consequently, a weapon has a place in the life of a believer. You might say that Peter received his "Carry License" from Jesus himself. And by extension, we have the same right.

In the Old Testament and the New, and specifically in the teaching of Jesus, we see that it is OK for God's people to have weapons for self-defense and for the defense of our families and our property. Thankfully, our Founding Fathers recognized that God-given right in the Second Amendment to the U.S. Constitution: "A well-regulated Militia, being necessary to the security of a free State, the right of the people to keep and bear Arms, shall not be infringed." While you still have that right in America, exercise it.

If you don't own a firearm, seriously consider buying one for protection, and be sure to get training on how to operate it safely. Founder George Washington said, "A free people ought not only to be armed, but disciplined."[5] Many gun retailers offer training, but there may be some great teachers in your church who would love to help. And once you are properly trained, you should train others in your home. Founder Richard Henry Lee said, "[T]o preserve liberty, it is essential that the whole body of the people always possess arms, and be taught alike, especially when young, how to use them."[6]

Even if every member of your family has a gun and is trained in how to use it defensively, when there is a threat, you must be the first into battle and ready to take a bullet. Before going to the cross, Jesus declared: "Greater love has no one than this, that someone lay down his life for his friends" (John 15:13). He demonstrated that supreme love for us when he was taken to the place of the skull, nailed to that cruel cross, and died so that we might have life. Men, he is our model. We should be willing to lay down our lives in defense of our families.

Defend against Defeat – Joshua 7:1–26

Caught red-handed! Kenyn tells the story of what happened:

My mom was changing the sheets on my bed when she noticed a lump in the mattress. She lifted the edge and discovered my stash. As a fourteen-year-old, my thirteen-year-old cousin had introduced me to pornography. He had found some magazines in my maternal grandfather's bottom dresser drawer. I was now fifteen and had amassed quite a collection. My mom was horrified and immediately showed one of the magazines to my father. I remained clueless that I had been found out until my dad was driving me to the high school one morning.

Dad pulled up to the school, parked, and turned off the engine. "Son, before you get out, I need to say something to you." My heart sank. I had a feeling I knew what it was about. "Your mother found pornography under your mattress." My worst fears were confirmed. I'm sure I looked like I had been shot. He continued: "You made a profession of faith and were baptized. We have you in church every Sunday, and we talk about the

Word and have prayer around our table. Do you think your Lord would be pleased about this?" My voice broke when I replied, "No, sir." He said, "Well I am disappointed in you, son. And I will not have that filth in my house. The Bible says, 'He that covereth his sins shall not prosper: but whoso confesseth and forsaketh them shall have mercy' (Prov. 28:13 KJV). So get rid of those magazines, make things right with the Lord, and never do that again. You understand me?" I replied, "Yes, sir."

I stepped out of that old Chevy Blazer stunned, my spirit crushed under the weight of my guilt and my dad's disappointment. I am grateful God used my dad to confront me in my sin, reminding me of the consequences and pointing the way back to forgiveness. I am thankful that my dad took seriously his role as a defender against spiritual defeat in our home. He dealt with sin in our family.

Joshua and the people of Israel had just experienced the thrill of victory when God brought down the walls of Jericho in chapter 6, but in chapter 7 they tasted the agony of defeat because there was sin in the camp. "But the people of Israel broke faith in regard to the devoted things, for Achan the son of Carmi, son of Zabdi, son of Zerah, of the tribe of Judah, took some of the devoted things. And the anger of the LORD burned against the people of Israel" (7:1). This is God's editorial comment. What is he talking about here? Go back to chapter 6:18: "But you, keep yourselves from the things devoted to destruction, lest when you have devoted them you take any of the devoted things and make the camp of Israel a thing for destruction and bring trouble upon it." And that's what they did (v. 24). God gave them a great victory at Jericho. Some of the spoils were devoted to destruction and burned, while other spoils were to be taken into the Lord's treasury. And if anyone took any of the spoils, God said that person will bring destruction down upon himself and on Israel.

God wants us to live in continual victory, but here God's people experienced an embarrassing defeat. How could such a thing happen? There was sin in the camp. So as we study this episode in Joshua, let's look at it from two perspectives as men. First, look through the eyes of Achan, who brought death to himself and his family and defeat to Israel. Second, look through the eyes of Joshua, who had to defend against defeat.

Achan, the Perpetrator

Just for a moment, slide into Achan's sandals. Imagine what it would have been like. You've just had a victory celebration, for the formidable city of Jericho has fallen. Praises have been sung, sacrifices have been offered, and merriment has been made. Many items of gold and silver have been collected and placed in the Lord's treasury. But now it's late, and every man has gone into his own tent. And there is the empty hulk of the city of Jericho, smoldering in the moonlight. All is quiet, all are asleep, except for one man. Achan opens the flap of his tent, and looks this way and that way, and then slips out under the cover of darkness. He climbs over the rubble and charred remains of what was the city of Jericho. He picks his way through the jumble of timbers and stones, and suddenly, he steps on something and hears a familiar clink. He uncovers in the ashes and blackened dirt a scorched leather pouch. He pulls it open and sees a couple hundred shekels of silver . . . more money than he's ever held in his whole life! And he stands there and lets the coins flow though his fingers like water. Then he pours it into his leather pouch and shoves it down into his tunic.

He goes a little further and stumbles over something that looks like a wedge of cheese in the moonlight. A broad smile forms on his face; his feverish fingers try to pull it free, but it burns to the touch. So he tears off a strip of his robe and uses that to pick up a big wedge of gold, still hot from the fire. He quickly wraps it up and drops that into his pouch and moves on. And a little further, he spies something else shining in the rubble. He tugs at it and pulls it out from under a pile of dust and soot. He shakes it out, and it's a beautiful, jewel-encrusted, multi-colored Babylonian robe. *A robe fit for a king!* he thought. Achan rolls it up and places that in his bag as well.

In a few hours it will be daylight, so he picks his way back through the rubble and sneaks back into the camp of Israel and to his tent where his family is sleeping. He is so excited that he cannot help but wake them and tell them the news and show them his treasure, hush their excitement, and swear them to secrecy. But instead of turning this treasure over to the priests to be placed in the Lord's treasury as the Lord commanded, making sure no one sees him, Achan pulls back his bed roll and digs a hole in the dirt floor of his tent, while his family congratulates him. And there he carefully places his stolen treasure, covers it up, smoothes out his bed roll, lays down with a big smile on his face, and stretches out for an hour of sleep. He thinks he's gotten away with it. Nobody outside of his family knew that he had done it . . . except God. God knew there was sin in the camp.

Morning came early for Achan and his family. He was awakened by the sound of the trumpet, calling for the fighting men to assemble. They are going again into battle. The next military target had been spied out, and it is determined that only 3,000 hand-picked men would be needed to take a small village named Ai. Since it is not a walled city like Jericho, certainly it would be easy prey for God's victorious army. But when Israel's forces attack, the men of Ai turn on the people of God, and they are routed. In all, thirty-six Hebrew soldiers lost their lives, but it could have been much worse. And it all happened because there was sin in the camp.

Now there was an individual who committed the sin, but not only did God hold that man accountable and his family accountable as co-conspirators, but he held the whole nation of Israel accountable. Look at 7:10–11: "The LORD said to Joshua, 'Get up! Why have you fallen on your face? Israel has sinned . . . .'" Did you get that? Israel has sinned. Someone might say: "Wait a minute, I thought there was a man named Achan who sinned?" He did. However, does God hold a whole nation accountable for one man's sin? There's a sense in which he does. For example, the husband is the head of the home, the representative of the home. The king is the representative of the nation. And God holds the representative responsible for the whole. That's why God called out Adam and not Eve in Genesis 3, because Adam as the head of the house was held primarily responsible. The same is true of the king. In his pride, David took a census and numbered the people, and God judged the nation as a whole for David's sin (1 Chron. 21).

Consider also the fact God will hold us accountable as Christians and citizens for the moral and spiritual condition of this nation. Few would argue that the national sin of slavery impacted the entire country with an estimated 650,000 casualties in the Civil War.[7] Do we dare question whether or not God will hold us all accountable for the national sin of abortion? Listen, Christians are partly responsible. We need to own it. It happened on our watch. When you read some of the prayers in the Word of God, especially those of Nehemiah and Daniel, they confess the sins of their fathers as if they themselves had committed them. So there's a sense in which God holds us to account for the sinful actions of others.

But what about the guy who caused all this trouble? What about Achan? What was the root cause of his sin? Look at Joshua 7:21: "When I saw among the spoil a beautiful cloak from Shinar, and 200 shekels of silver, and a bar of gold weighing 50 shekels, then I coveted them and took them." Underline that word "coveted." What is covetousness? Covetousness is an inordinate desire for things that are not rightfully ours. Things that we have no right to. God graciously promises to provide for our needs, but not our "greeds."

Listen to the warning of Jesus in Luke 12:15: "Take care, and be on your guard against all covetousness, for one's life does not consist in the abundance of his possessions." And yet America is a shallow society obsessed with having an abundance of things. We buy things for the house, things for the bedroom, things for the bathroom, things for the den, things for the living room, things for the kitchen, things for the garage, things to put in things in, things to put things on. And then we insure all those things. And when we get tired of those things, we have a garage sale or put these things on Facebook or eBay, to pass those things to somebody else and get a little money to buy new things.

The apostle Paul had the right view of things. He said: "Forgetting what lies behind" (Phil. 3:13); "Giving thanks always and for *everything*" (Eph. 5:20, emphasis added); "Whatever is true, whatever is honorable, whatever is just, whatever is pure, whatever is lovely, whatever is commendable, if there is any excellence, if there is *anything* worthy of praise, think about these *things*" (Phil. 4:8, emphasis added). Why? Because the day is going to come when you are going to die, and the only *thing* in that box is going to be you!

Don't let the desire for possessions possess you like it did Achan. Don't get us wrong—it is OK to have things, but at some point our relationship with possessions can become unhealthy. Teach your children the story of Achan as an illustration of how a man as the head of the household and defender of his family can bring judgment on his whole family.

Pornography, the Destroyer

Your hidden sin may not be the same as Achan's. Maybe you identify with Kenyn's sin from the opening story. Perhaps your secret sin is pornography. Statistically, if you are a man reading our words right now, you are more likely than not viewing porn at least occasionally.[8] Some are struggling with a serious addiction to it. Only one in twenty (5 percent) of porn users say it sometimes hurts their relationships,[9] but they are fooling themselves. Believe us, it will ruin your intimacy with your wife, and estrangement from your wife will hurt your children. Don't be more committed to your sin than to your family. Josh McDowell began his ministry as a defender of the faith, but now he is laser-focused on battling the porn epidemic that is destroying families and morally eviscerating the church. He offers "10 Ways to Fight Pornography":[10]

1. Admit you have a problem: We live in a world that wants us to make allowance for justifying and tolerating almost every off-color thing we can think of. One of the best things you can do for yourself, your marriage, and your children is to admit you have a problem with pornography.

2. Invite trusted friends to encourage you and hold you accountable. We would also suggest bringing your wife in on your struggle. Voicing your struggle to others and admitting you have a problem is a huge step in the right direction.

3. Online accountability. Use software to monitor your online activity. Covenant Eyes is a great resource for men. It allows you to receive your accountability partner's reports weekly for the sites they visit and the searches they make. It lets you know when you need to follow up with each other on questionable activity. Finally, it allows you to celebrate with each other in putting online struggles to death.

4. Set boundaries with your mobile device. Nowadays, our smartphones and tablets are even more of a gateway to pornography than a desktop computer. The same online accountability applies to your mobile device. Set boundaries and use software to monitor all online activity.

5. If you have offline pornography at your disposal, destroy it. If you are wanting to fight your addiction to pornography but are hanging on to that magazine or DVD (in its secret hiding place) then your "fight" is really just a masquerade. Man up, and destroy those items. Right now.

6. Take all forms of media seriously. Don't think to yourself that TV shows or movies that emphasize sexual situations or portray women in the wrong light are harmless. Even if they are not considered "porn," they are damaging. If you're struggling with pornography, these types of entertainment will only make your struggle more difficult.

7. If you are married, take a step back and think on your marriage. Are you satisfied and happy in your marriage? What's awesome about your marriage? What is lacking? Are you content with the level of sexual intimacy within your marriage? These are great questions to ask yourself. They just might lead you to the root cause for your addiction.

8. Realize that you didn't just become addicted to porn. How you conduct yourself in public and where you look every day have greatly influenced where you find yourself today. That long stare at the passing woman, the double take at the lady you just walked by, the thoughts that come to mind when you see the magazines in the checkout lane at the grocery store . . . . This is where the battle starts in the everyday scenarios and situations. Fight the good fight here too. Guard your eyes and guard your mind.

9. Take a second and think beyond the images or videos you're looking at. This is a person, a real woman, a human being created by God, just like you. She's somebody's daughter, sister, or even mother. Think of what her life must be like in front of the camera day after day—exploited and made insanely vulnerable.

Chances are she is wrapped up in some kind of string of human sex trafficking, and your addiction is helping to fund this multi-billion-dollar business. She is not there for your enjoyment. She is being held captive, and more than likely is crying out for help.

10. Your pornography addiction is a heart issue first and foremost. You are exchanging truth for a lie. You are voluntarily placing your affections on the cheap thrills that are ultimately fleeting and leave you feeling worthless. You were created for God, by God. Ask God to help you every time you are tempted.

Collateral Damage

Maybe your struggle is not with pornography. However, regardless of your secret sin, it has far-reaching consequences. The consequences of Achan's sin were severe:

- It dishonored God (vv. 8–9).
- It brought defeat to his brothers (v. 12).
- It brought disgrace to his parents (v. 17).
- It brought death to his loved ones (vv. 24–25).

The point is this: our sin is not just a self-inflicted wound. It creates collateral damage that impacts those around us. As the Bible says: "For none of us lives to himself, and none of us dies to himself" (Rom. 14:7). A godly husband protects his family by turning from personal sin and pursuing holiness. Again, a man cannot commit himself to sin without his whole family bearing consequences. Sometimes the greatest gift you can give your family is a silent, hidden decision to refrain from pursuing sin. When our sin is exposed, we also reduce our credibility as an instructor, especially when we have a sinful flaw such as porn in our lives. So out of love for your wife and children, resist temptation, flee sin, and pursue a path back to holiness. In this way you will be protecting your family from your sin and from the effects of your sin.

Joshua, the Defender

Let's look briefly at Joshua, who is primarily a positive example for us as men. First, notice that as soon as Joshua learned of the army's defeat, he humbled himself and cried out to the Lord:

> Then Joshua tore his clothes and fell to the earth on his face before the ark of the LORD until the evening, he and the elders of Israel. And they put dust on their heads. And Joshua said, "Alas, O Lord GOD, why have you brought this people over the Jordan at all, to give us into the hands of the Amorites, to destroy us? Would that we had been content to dwell beyond the Jordan! O Lord, what can I say, when Israel has turned their backs before their enemies! For the Canaanites and all the inhabitants of the land will hear of it and will surround us and cut off our name from the earth. And what will you do for your great name?" (7:6–9)

Then God tells him what has happened and what he needs to do: get up off your face, assemble the people, ID the perpetrator, and execute justice (vv. 10–15). That, my friends, was the proverbial swift kick in the seat of Joshua's pants by God. Ever had that happen to you? We have, and it was just what we needed at the time to get up and put on our armor and charge back into battle. In fact, Joshua follows God's instructions to the letter. Joshua gathers the people, confronts Achan, makes him confess, and carries out the sentence of death.

Several principles immediately surface for men. First, when we learn of sin in our "camp," our initial response should be to humble ourselves before God and ask for his help as the leader responsible to deal with it. Then there needs to be a personal confrontation and call for confession. Remind the offender of the verse Kenyn's dad quoted—Proverbs 28:13: "Whoever conceals his transgressions will not prosper, but he who confesses and forsakes them will obtain mercy." Finally, there needs to be some sort of disciplinary consequence. When kids are young, sometimes it means the application of the "board of education to the seat of knowledge" as the old grade-school teachers called it (i.e., a swat on the backside). When they get older, you need to be creative, like withholding whatever they value most. Regardless, let Galatians 6:1 be your guide: "Brothers, if anyone is caught in any transgression, you who are spiritual should restore him in a spirit of gentleness." So don't discipline out of anger, otherwise you risk another danger, as Paul points out: "Fathers, do not provoke your children, lest they become discouraged" (Col. 3:21). It is possible to take discipline too far, and you need to know that every child is different. For some, it just takes a look or a harsh word to break their spirit. For others, it takes much more. At the end of the day, take Ephesians 6:4 as a goal: "Fathers, do not provoke your children to anger, but bring them up in the discipline and instruction of the Lord."

There is more to being a defender than simply being the first down the stairs when there is a noise in the night. You must develop a "situational awareness" of what is happening both inside and outside of your home and constantly be on guard against the dangers and temptations your family may encounter. Further, the old maxim, "The Best Defense Is a Strong Offense" applies here. For example, you will be proactive in monitoring and controlling your family's media intake. That means you will need to take the lead in ensuring that your children have guardrails on their internet access, blocking pornography or access to other questionable material. You will need to develop a plan to defend your children from predators online or offline by limiting social media interaction. Obviously, you will do your best to ensure that they are not encountering things that their minds and hearts are not yet equipped to understand or handle. You will vet the video games they want to buy or play with friends. You will not only instruct your children in God's plan for properly expressing themselves sexually in the context of a marriage relationship, but also guard and protect your children from sexual temptation or sexual expression while they are dating. The godly husband protects his wife and children by helping them flee sin so they do not suffer its painful consequences. Seek to guard your family from their own sin.

Protect the Powerless – Joshua 10:1–11

This idea of being a defender isn't simply about being protective of your wife or your children or your family—although that's certainly a major part of it. It's really about who God made you to be as a man. You were made to be a warrior from the womb. And you're probably going to have more than a few opportunities to take action to defend someone other than a family member just by living in today's messed-up world where people are downright mean to each other.

At this point in the book of Joshua, God had already given Jericho to Israel, and after they dealt with the sin in the camp, God gave them Ai and then they renewed the covenant. As you might imagine, the word spread about another fallen city, and the fear of God fell over the people in that land. This was a highly significant battle because it marked the turning point in the conquest of Canaan. In chapter 9, we found that the various tribes of people decided to get together and form an alliance against Israel. Again, all the "-ites" stopped fighting each other long enough to fight against Joshua.

Remember how the Gibeonites sent a delegation, pretending as if they were from a far-off country who had heard of Israel's mighty God? Old Joshua must have been a sucker for a sob story because he fell for it, even though God had told him before he crossed the Jordan River that he was to kill all the inhabitants of Canaan. Furthermore, he made a treaty with the Gibeonites, promised to protect them, and brought these men into their camp. Well, the truth came out. Some of the people wanted the Gibeonites destroyed, but Joshua and the leaders took the blame and said: "We gave our word; we must keep our word." The Bible speaks of a man who takes a vow to his own hurt and yet he keeps it (Psalm 15:4), and Joshua was a man of his word. Consequently, the Gibeonites were spared, but they were relegated to become Israel's water boys and woodcutters.

Now in chapter 10, we join the "termite" alliance already in progress, and five kings are making their battle plans against Joshua. They heard about the double-cross deal the Gibeonites worked with Israel, and they're mad. So they gather their troops and march against the Gibeonites. The Gibeonites then send an urgent message to Joshua: "Hey, don't forget the treaty we made with you—don't abandon us! Save us! Help us!" So Joshua, true to his word, brought up his entire army from Gilgal, marched them all night for fifteen miles over rough country, and they caught these five kings and their army by surprise. And the Lord threw them into confusion, and they began to retreat, which is a dignified way of saying they ran for their lives.

And as the sun reached high noon, the five kings' army in disarray and in flight, they try to escape through a narrow pass. Joshua, being the general he is, knows he has the enemy right where he wants them. This is a golden opportunity to break the back of any kind of organized alliance against him—this is a strategic moment. And looking back, he was right, because this battle was the *coup de grâce*; it sounded the death knell; it marked the beginning of the end of the conquest of Canaan. Everything else was downhill after this battle. Joshua realized this, but he needed more time to get the job done. So Joshua prophetically and prayerfully says: "Sun, stand still at Gibeon, and moon, in the Valley of Aijalon" (10:12). And sure enough, time seemed to stand still. The sun stopped coursing through the sky. The moon hung motionless over the valley of Aijalon. And the day was extended for Joshua so God could give them an awesome victory!

With God's help, Joshua and the armies of Israel defended the defenseless and protected the powerless Gibeonites. Mission accomplished! Well, that was then—what about now? As you survey the cultural landscape, who needs defending?

Allow us to suggest a people group that is being slaughtered without mercy in America at an alarming rate. Of course, we are speaking of all the preborn babies who are killed through chemical and surgical abortions. Do you know what happens to these defenseless babies? Some abortionists inject the womb with a saline solution that burns and scalds the baby to death. Others stick a needle through the womb and into the baby's beating heart and inject it with poison that kills the child. Other abortionists use a vacuum device that dismembers and sucks the preborn baby's body parts out of the womb. Others use forceps, which the baby struggles to avoid, according to the sonograms. They rip off the limbs, crush the baby's head, pull the body out of the womb, and throw it in the trash! Or they harvest valuable organs before doing so as we have seen on undercover videos of Planned Parenthood personnel. And it happens every day in so-called "health clinics" and hospitals across America. Friends, this is diabolical savagery, yet we have a significant sector of our society that calls it a "choice."

Since the 1973 *Roe v. Wade* Supreme Court decision that granted a supposed constitutional right to abortion, over 60 million preborn babies have been terminated.[11] Let the weight of that hit you—over 60 million lives have been extinguished. Just think of a catastrophic disaster where the entire populations of California, Arizona, Nevada, Oregon, and Washington are wiped out. Gone! That is what we are talking about. Abortion is the American Holocaust, and it is a moral outrage that ought to make every Christian in this nation rise up in righteous indignation. That is especially true for men, who are called to defend the defenseless.

But don't just get mad, do something! Here are five practical ways to make a positive impact when it comes to defending and protecting preborn babies:

1. *Pray* that the dignity of every human life will be respected and protected from conception to natural death (Prov. 24:11–12).
2. *Encourage* your church leadership to speak to this issue biblically. There are many pro-life resources at **FRC.org/life**.
3. *Contact* your elected officials: Reach out to your representatives in the House and Senate by calling the U.S. Capitol switchboard at (202) 224-3121 or visit **FRCAction.org** and click "Contact Officials." Also, contact your state legislators. Urge them all to support legislation that protects human life. Tell the president to appoint pro-life justices and judges to the courts at **whitehouse.gov/contact**.
4. *Educate* yourself on pro-life arguments. Read the best arguments from science, the law, and women's rights to advance the pro-life case against abortion to your friends, family, and neighbors. To find out more about how to

promote the pro-life cause in your daily life, check out
FRC.org/life. Also check out "Pro-Life Apologetics for
the Next Generation" by Scott Klusendorf.[12]

5. *Support* a pregnancy care center in your area. To find
   out if there is a life-affirming ministry to women in
   your area who are expecting a child or in need of post-
   abortive healing, check out **heartbeatinternational.org**
   for a directory.

There are obviously other groups of people who need
defending. For example, there are numerous biblical references
to defending the fatherless and the widow (e.g., Deut. 10:18;
Ps. 82:3; Isa. 1:17; James 1:27). Psalm 68:5 declares: "Father of
the fatherless and protector of widows is God in his holy hab-
itation." If that's how God identifies himself, and we are made
in his image, then we should act similarly. There are practical
ways we can help, like volunteering or giving to the local Boys &
Girls Club. As far as ministering to widows, if your church isn't
already doing something, get a group of guys together and make
a commitment to help ease their burden. For example, most
guys could help mow, trim hedges, rake leaves, maybe even do
simple car repairs like an oil change or rotate tires. Maybe you
have a lawyer in your church who could offer pro bono help to
defend a widow against fraud or a predatory lender.

In contemporary culture, we are increasingly made aware
of the multitudes of broken individuals who are victims of sex
trafficking. It is modern-day slavery. Anti–human trafficking
ministry A21 offers the following statistics:

- An estimated 20.9 to 45.8 million people are held in sex
  slavery today [worldwide].
- Approximately 71% of human trafficking victims are
  women and girls.

- Up to 50% of female victims are minors.
- Human trafficking generates an estimated USD $150.2 billion per year.
- Traffickers face a mere 1% chance of ever being prosecuted.[13]

Thankfully, there are a number of effective ministries dedicated to helping these girls and women escape this unbearable slavery, such as Samaritan's Purse, A21, Agape International Missions, International Justice Mission, and others (visit the coalition website: enditmovement.com). When we support ministries like these, we are helping to defend the defenseless. Can you name any other groups who need defending? Perhaps God is even placing a particular person on your heart right now. What are some practical things you can do to protect the defenseless?

We should also do what we can to protect the millions of brothers and sisters in Christ who are being persecuted. Scripture says, "Let brotherly love continue. . . . Remember those who are in prison, as though in prison with them, and those who are mistreated, since you also are in the body" (Heb. 13:1, 3). We can remember them by praying, which is powerful, but there are also practical things we can do, such as support hands-on efforts. There are a number of ministries offering relief to refugees, victims of violence, and the families of martyrs, such as Samaritan's Purse, Voice of the Martyrs, Open Doors USA, and others. Donate to these and other ministries. Volunteer your time to serve. Be the hands and heart of Christ to our persecuted brothers and sisters.

You get the picture. Defend the defenseless.

BATTLE BUDDY GROUP GUIDE

Week 4 – Man as Defender

▶ The Defender of the Defenseless
LTG (RET.) Jerry Boykin from his book *Man to Man*

Just before Thanksgiving in 2017, I was driving down the highway just north of Richmond. I was cruising along I-95 at about seventy-five miles an hour, when I saw a woman on the side of the road getting roughed up by a man. Alongside what appeared to be his car, I saw a man holding onto this woman by the hair. He was swinging her around in a circle and as I went by, he slammed her on the ground and kicked her. Then he sat on top of her and started punching.

I immediately pulled off the highway, steering in ahead of two more cars that had stopped between me and the assailant's vehicle. Both of those drivers were women, and it looked like they were both calling 911. Once I stopped, I reached over and grabbed my Kimber 1911 45-caliber pistol and I started to run along the edge of the highway to reach the assailant and stop him.

Of course, my mind was going at warp speed. *Do I shoot the guy, or do I try to knock him out with a pistol? What am I gonna do?* Thoughts were flying through my head faster than I could run.

My conclusion: I could live with standing before a judge, but I couldn't live with letting that thug kill the woman—and it looked very much like that's what he was trying to do. So right before I reached him, I raised my pistol. When he saw my gun, he scrambled off the woman. She struggled to her feet, clearly in a lot of pain, and moved slowly around the car to get out of his reach.

With the pistol pointed at his face, I backed him up against the car.

"What are you gonna do with that gun?" he asked. He was no fool and he realized the seriousness of the situation as he looked down the barrel of a 45-caliber pistol.

"I'm gonna shoot you if you touch that woman again." By then we both knew that I would use it if he made the wrong move.

Of course, I'm thinking, the only thing people driving down I-95 are going to remember was this white man jacking a round in the chamber of a pistol as he's running toward a black man.

Fortunately, the attacker's attitude changed quickly—just as a woman driving a Department of Transportation vehicle screeched to a halt. She had a badge and I said to myself, *Here we go. They're going to arrest me now, watch this . . . .*

But she didn't. Instead she said, "You hold him there while I check on her."

I stood right where I was and held the pistol on him. Apparently, the transportation officer had already received a full report, probably from one of the women who had called 911.

Then, while I was standing there holding the gun on the guy and the transportation officer was checking on the woman, two Virginia State Police pulled up.

I thought, *Well, this is it for sure.*

They walked over to me. I shoved my pistol into my belt, and said, "I have a concealed carry." One of them said, "Oh yeah, that's fine. Tell me what you saw here."

And that was the end of it—I filled them in on what had happened, and never heard from them again.

The point was, I couldn't drive by and not do something about what was going on—I *had* to do something to stop it. First of all, I'm a man. Second, somebody had to help that woman, or her abuser was probably going to kill her. Turned out he had already broken her ribs. Third, why do I have a concealed carry permit if not for that kind of situation? To stop a woman from possibly being killed and certainly being battered.[14] ◀

Group Debrief

At some point in our lives, most of us will face a situation where we must take a risk to defend the defenseless—whether that means putting our life, our reputation, or something else on the line. We may not encounter a situation as crazy as the one outlined in the story above, but we will almost certainly face a situation that involves protecting the vulnerable. Don't think so? Just think about our own society. In several states across America, it is legal to kill an unborn baby up to the day of their birth! Proverbs 24:10–12 is a great wake-up call to action:

> If you do nothing in a difficult time, your strength is limited. Rescue those being taken off to death, and save those stumbling toward slaughter. If you say, "But we didn't know about this," won't he who weighs hearts consider it? Won't he who protects your life know? Won't he repay a person according to his work? (CSB)

Questions to Consider

- Have you ever faced a situation similar to the one General Jerry Boykin faced in this story? If so, how did you react? If not, do you think you would have the courage to take action in such a situation?

- What would you have to do to put yourself in a situation to respond in a way to make a positive difference?

- What can you do to help protect the vulnerable, both on a daily basis, and in situations of crisis?

- What might protecting the defenseless cost you? Is it worth it? Why?

CHAPTER 5

Man as a Battle Buddy

General Boykin recounts how Army recruits are assigned a "battle buddy" during their training. The idea is to pair up with another recruit for the purpose of comradery, mutual encouragement, and accountability. The elite Rangers use this battle buddy system better than any other military organization, because their operations are generally very high-risk, and knowing that your buddy is watching your flank is not only useful but also comforting. In a combat situation, having a reliable battle buddy can mean the difference between life and death. He's got your back and you've got his. The battle buddy concept has served our soldiers well for decades. In fact, it works across the board. Men need other men to survive, let alone be successful, as a man. In this chapter, we will explore what the book of Joshua has to teach us about the value of connecting with a friend who becomes a battle buddy, the necessity of holding other men accountable, and the need to mentor another man.

Friendship Forged in the Fire – Joshua 14:6–15

Dog-tired and dirty from head to toe, I (Cureton) stepped into the shower when I heard a loud knock on my front door. I ignored it. And for good reason, because I had just unloaded all our worldly goods into our seminary apartment by myself, then got under the truck I had towed and reconnected the U-Joint. I had grease and grime all over me, and you don't have to have much imagination to know what I smelled like. Oh, and that was after driving sixteen hours the day before from east Tennessee to Fort Worth, Texas. As I put my head under the refreshing stream of hot water and reached for the soap, there was another knock—this time louder and longer. At that point, I was getting steamed—and not from the shower. But I turned off the water, stepped out wet, wrapped a towel around my waist when yet another knock came, but this time it was with pounding and shouting: "Hellooo! Hey, are you in there?! Anybody home?!"

It was a good thing I was at a seminary because I was about to lose my religion . . . . I gritted my teeth, picked up my sweat-soaked, greasy, nasty clothes, pulled them on, and looked out the peep hole, and there he was: big smile, full of energy and enthusiasm, brimming with Tennessee pride, and, as I learned later, a passion to tell people about Jesus. Anyway, I grudgingly opened the door, and he opened his mouth and out came a torrent:

"Hey, my name is David; man, we are glad to have you here, and I saw your Tennessee tags. Hey, I'm from Tennessee too! Our apartment is right over there. Good to have another Volunteer fan here. So what part of Tennessee are y'all from?" And then he took his first breath. "You're married, right? Is your wife with you? Have any kids? I guess not because that is a one bedroom, right? What degree program are you doing?"

And on and on he went while I stood there in the doorway looking like I had a wrestling match with a greased gorilla and lost. Little did I know then that I had just met the man who would become my closest battle buddy.

David and I are a part of a Christian denomination that had drifted toward liberalism, and we became foot soldiers in what was called the "conservative resurgence." It was a theological conflict that consumed our tribe for about twenty years, and at the end of the day, we moved it back to the foundational belief in the inerrant Word of God as the final authority for faith and practice. Our friendship was forged in the fire being brothers-in-arms.

As a young pastor, David let me preach in his church, which led to another little church in the same area of north Texas calling me as pastor. We had the shared experience of leading our first congregations in neighboring communities, as well as engaging in the broader denominational battles.

Additionally, our bond was deepened when he nearly lost his wife who was expecting and delivered prematurely. My wife and I spent many hours in the hospital, watching his other little daughter, praying with them and for them and helping out as we could, while David and his wife and newborn child went through the fight of their lives. Thankfully, both pulled through but with lifelong health challenges. Walking with David through all of that has made us battle buddies for life.

Now over thirty years later, we live in different states, hundreds of miles apart, but we talk and text regularly. We get together a couple of times a year, usually when he and his family are driving back through Tennessee to visit family over holidays or to enjoy a UT football game. And it is amazing how we pick right up where we left off. I know that if I need David, he will drop everything and be there for me. He knows the same. He has my back and I have his.

God connected me with David, and God certainly connected Joshua with Caleb. These two warriors went way back . . . at least forty years back. What do we know about Caleb? His name in ancient Near Eastern languages means "dog." It was a name intended to reflect "loyalty and faithfulness to his master." How appropriate for this man. In fact, based on his unwavering loyalty and unparalleled faithfulness, God added this description: "*My servant* Caleb" (Num. 14:24, emphasis added), a title of highest honor God reserved only for the greatest of leaders, like Moses himself. Caleb was a legend in his own time. Today we're still naming our children after Joshua and his battle buddy Caleb.

We meet this remarkable warrior in Numbers 13. Liberated by God from Egyptian slavery with signs and wonders, his people miraculously passed through the Red Sea, wound their way through a wilderness, moved into position on the edge of the promised land, and God instructed Moses: "Send men to scout out the land of Canaan I am giving to the Israelites. Send one man who is a leader among them from each of their ancestral tribes" (Num. 13:2 csb). Twelve exceptional men were chosen to run this long-range reconnaissance mission. Each of the twelve selected for his leadership, this group also likely possessed superior physical capabilities, fighting skills, and the ability to thrive behind enemy lines. The twelve tribes of Israel ran their "selection and assessment" process, and the best "Delta" or "Force Recon" or "SEAL" from each tribe was carefully chosen for this particularly dangerous operation. They were such outstanding individuals that their names are listed in an exceptional unit roster in Numbers 13.

The best of these twelve, a member of the tribe of Ephraim, was appointed as team leader. We meet him as Hoshea, the son of Nun. Moses called him "Joshua," the name we remember him by and the focus of this book. Joshua's assistant team leader was Caleb. Their mission, essentially the same for all recon teams in every age, was to scout out the land—to evaluate its characteristics, appraise its strategic value, measure its military strength, and particularly assess its fortifications. They were to bring back actionable intelligence regarding the land's occupants, who would be their opponents. What a tremendous responsibility these twelve men carried. The future of the Jewish people rested with them and their ability to facilitate a successful capture of the "promised land." The question was whether they were up to the task.

The mission lasted for several weeks. As it turned out, ten members of that original team lost their nerve somewhere between their departure and their return to friendly lines. Seeing with their own eyes the intimidating numbers of indigenous defense forces, the daunting type of fortified cities, and the scary size of some of the enemy warriors, these ten hit the panic button, tucked tail, tapped out, and reported that God had given them a "mission impossible." They declared: "We can't do it . . . they are too strong . . . the land would swallow us up . . . they're giants and we are only grasshoppers next to them" (see Num. 13:28, 31–33). Not surprisingly, their report struck fear into the hearts of the entire nation.

However, two of the twelve—Joshua and Caleb—saw things differently, and they delivered a diametrically opposite, God-oriented, hope-filled, and confident report. They professed that not only had God given them a "mission possible," but a mission that would be successful. Consequently, Caleb boldly declared: "Let's go up now and take possession of the land because we can certainly conquer it!" (Num. 13:30 CSB).

Caleb and Joshua viewed reality by faith and not by sight, fed off each other's courage, and were intensely loyal to God and to one another. Neither of these men would disgrace himself in the presence of the other by showing himself a coward. After all, they were battle buddies, and that meant there was no turning back or letting each other down, because they had agreed to depend on God and on each other.

Just think how differently the history of Israel could have played out if Moses had sent only these two men and if their report had been received! They gave each other the kind of mutual support they greatly needed when their fellow team members fell prey to cowardice. Caleb and Joshua stood together and encouraged the people to launch the invasion of Canaan immediately. What the ten sorely lacked, the two displayed big time. Joshua and Caleb were characterized by an unconquerable faith and fortitude. The reason? These men were united in their view of their great God, which made those fortified cities look vulnerable, fiery battles winnable, and a fierce enemy beatable— yes, even the giants.

Fast-forward forty-five years later to our text in Joshua 14. With the help of their God, these two battle buddies had experienced many victories and only one defeat at Ai, and even that was reversed. There were more battles to come, but by the time we get to the end of chapter 13, the main-force opposition had been broken. Now only the toughest enemy strongholds remained. So in chapter 14, the land is mostly in Israel's control. This last and most difficult part of the campaign is the background for Caleb's conversation with Joshua in 14:6–14. Picture these two seasoned warriors sitting around a campfire in the desert on a starry night before they and their troops cross the line of departure for this final major mission together. Let's listen in and learn more about what it means to be a battle buddy:

> The descendants of Judah approached Joshua at Gilgal, and Caleb son of Jephunneh the Kenizzite said to him, "You know what the Lord promised Moses the man of God at Kadesh-barnea about you and me. I was forty years old when Moses the Lord's servant sent me from Kadesh-barnea to scout the land, and I brought back an honest report. My brothers who went with me caused the people to lose heart, but I followed the Lord my God completely. On that day Moses swore to me: 'The land where you have set foot will be an inheritance for you and your

descendants forever, because you have followed the LORD my God completely."

"As you see, the LORD has kept me alive these forty-five years as he promised, since the LORD spoke this word to Moses while Israel was journeying in the wilderness. Here I am today, eighty-five years old. I am still as strong today as I was the day Moses sent me out. My strength for battle and for daily tasks is now as it was then. Now give me this hill country the LORD promised me on that day, because you heard then that the Anakim are there, as well as large fortified cities. Perhaps the Lord will be with me and I will drive them out as the Lord promised."

Then Joshua blessed Caleb son of Jephunneh and gave him Hebron as an inheritance. Therefore, Hebron still belongs to Caleb son of Jephunneh the Kenizzite as an inheritance today because he followed the Lord, the God of Israel, completely. (vv. 6–14 CSB)

"You and Me"

"You know what the LORD promised Moses the man of God at Kadesh-barnea . . ." (v. 6b).

Here Caleb draws upon some shared history. He relates the current situation to its historical roots, bringing the past to bear upon the present. This phrase in the text can also be rendered, "Remember what the LORD said" (Josh. 14:6 NLT)—a deliberate recalling of the path these men had walked together from that critical moment.

". . . you and me" (v. 6c).

Just three little words—and we often repeat these same words too casually, even flippantly. But there's nothing casual or flippant here for Caleb. He and Joshua know each other. They've been soldiering together for nearly a half-century. There's a long track record of blood and battle scars, of facing enormous difficulties together, of experiencing victory after victory together. By now these two war-seasoned veterans knew each other especially well, having been battle buddies for years, both spiritually and militarily. These men had fought side-by-side in at least six major battles before they even entered the promised land. Since then, they had been on numerous missions together. So there is nearly a lifetime of loyalty behind those words. "You and me, Joshua" reflects a full career of battlefield allegiance, camaraderie, and shared hardship and danger. These two old soldiers have had each other's backs for decades now. Once more these battle buddies are poised to step into the fray—together.

Warfare in the ancient Near East was mostly *mano a mano*. Bows and arrows, spears and javelins, swords and shields powered by biceps and triceps, pecs and delts, gluts and quads. Human muscle was coupled with lethal weapons and a lot of courage, grit, and determination. It was a dog-eat-dog, survival-of-the-fittest culture. And the biggest dogs were usually the biggest winners. In such a world, for a man to be battle-fit for more than a decade took some doing. Military "careers" tended to be short-lived more often than not. Not so with Caleb.

According to verse 10, Caleb is now a remarkable age eighty-five—but he wasn't your typical senior citizen. Caleb was still a strong and courageous man, a force to be reckoned with in combat on the battlefield. He wasn't bragging but stating facts when he declared: "I am still as strong today as I was the day Moses sent me out. My strength for battle and for daily tasks is now as it was then" (v. 11 csb). You might say that Caleb was an iron man before there was an Iron Age. Caleb was the Tom Brady of the ancient Israeli Defense Force and destined for its Hall of Fame. When it came to the battlefield, Caleb was indeed in the running for G.O.A.T. And the only friendly competition was his battle buddy Joshua.

And even now Caleb isn't ready to retire; he is ready for a real challenge. He is itching for a fight: "Give me this mountain" (KJV), he asks of his battle buddy Joshua. And yes, it was one of the toughest assignments left on the map. There are giants and large fortified cities there. Yet it was the place God had promised him. And with that promise came the hope of God's presence: "Perhaps the LORD will be with me and I will drive them out as the LORD promised" (v. 12 CSB).

Notice Caleb didn't presume on God; he said, "Perhaps . . . ." Caleb is confident, not cocky. By saying "perhaps," he fully realizes he may not survive the next battle. He may never get a chance to embrace his wife, hug his kids, or hold his grandbabies again. Caleb knew he might march up that mountain, but he may never come back alive. Such is the lot and life of a warrior. He and Joshua understood that well. They had buried many fellow soldiers along the way. At the end of the day, old Caleb understood that even his exceptional physical fitness, fighting skill, and fortitude would only carry the day if God was with him and enabled him to prevail. He and Joshua were alike in that. Above all they trusted in their God.

You can almost see and hear Caleb and Joshua having this exchange. They experienced a battlefield solidarity among soldiers that defies description. Doubtless their love and respect for one another was incredible. Here they are on the eve of another campaign, the last major one for Caleb. In the light of the flickering campfire, you can almost see the fire in Caleb's eyes as he relishes the fight; you can almost hear the confidence he has in their God; you can almost sense the camaraderie between these two battle buddies as Caleb speaks from his heart to Joshua: "You and me, old friend. You and me, against all odds, against walled cities, against giants. You and me, for God and country.

You and me, with heaven's help and no holding back. You and me, one more time, together!"

"You and me . . ." simple but powerful words and the essence of the battle buddy relationship with another man.

Blessing and Affirmation

How did Joshua respond to his old friend, his battle buddy? He blessed him. He affirmed Caleb. He brought God into the mix. No doubt Joshua prayed over him and asked God to go with Caleb on his mission, God to watch over him in battle, God to make his sword swift and his aim sure, and God to crown his efforts with victory. He blessed and affirmed Caleb.

How we need affirmation from other men in our culture. Rather than being lampooned in sitcoms and minimized as the butt of jokes, men need to affirm each other. Maybe your friend is facing the fight of his life. Some major life challenge: physical, spiritual, financial, marital, whatever. That is the time to say: "Brother, I want to bless you, ask God to intervene on your behalf, give you the strength to endure, and if need be, carry you through it."

Michael, my (Cureton's) best friend growing up and first battle buddy, recently lost his brother. The man literally died in Michael's arms after suffering a massive heart attack. Michael had done all he could . . . called 911, tried to perform CPR, and he cried out to God. But his brother was gone. Though his brother was a believer, Michael was devastated. He picked up the phone and called me while I was in Colorado as we were winding up our Stand Courageous Conference. Even though we were really tight as teenagers and young men, it had been a few years since I had seen him or spoke with him. Weeping, he related the bad news via voice mail and simply asked for my prayers. But I hopped on an early morning flight back home to be with my battle buddy.

When I made it to him, we hugged each other, his tears flowing freely. He unfolded how it all played out, how he felt helpless, and he confessed, "I don't know what I'm going to do without my brother." So I prayed for him. I blessed him. I asked God to stand with him and hold him up, give him the strength to endure, and if need be, to carry him through this season of sorrow. We hugged again, and he said, "I love you, brother."

I replied, "I love you. If there's anything, I mean anything—"

He stopped me with "I know . . . you just being here and praying over me means the world to me."

It has been over forty years since Michael and I were in high school together, went fishing together, and hung out together for any length of time. We've stayed in touch sporadically through the years. But when you have a battle buddy, time and distance apart means very little when he is hurting and in need. Battle buddies drop everything to stand with you in a fight, affirm you when you need encouragement, and pray over and bless you as you take on life's challenges. That's what Joshua did for Caleb. That's what we need to do for our battle buddies.

As Iron Sharpens Iron – Joshua 7:16–20; 9:22–27; 22:10–34

Our (Cureton's) phone rang on a rainy November Saturday afternoon in north Texas. Mom and Dad back in Tennessee were on the line. We caught up like we did every week, hearing mostly from Mom about the latest happenings back home, and I would share a snapshot of our work week and my studies. When the newsy part of the conversation wound down, Dad would take the phone and say, "OK son, ready to sharpen swords?"

"Got my Bible open and ready," I replied.

Then we would dive in and tackle some knotty topics from the Scriptures. Occasionally, we would find ourselves on opposite sides of the interpretation or the application. Sometimes the conversation would get intense, even heated. But these sessions not only deepened my knowledge of Scripture but also taught me how to defend my position. We called it "sharpening swords," which is a nod to Proverbs 27:17: "Iron sharpens iron, and one man sharpens another."

I miss those priceless times with my dad. Through the years, I have had other "sword sharpening" buddies. Thankfully, I now have a son-in-law to spar with. He just finished his seminary degree, assumed his first pastorate, but he has different views and perspectives on some doctrines. Needless to say, the young man keeps me fresh and continually studying. He makes me a better man. I trust I am doing the same for him—iron sharpening iron. What about you? Do you have another man with whom you are "sharpening swords"?

When a battle buddy or family member blows it, you don't always have the luxury of "letting it go" or "letting him slide." Sometimes you have to love him enough to call him out and confront him. There's too much at stake.

General Boykin's battle buddy Stu Weber admits: "I wouldn't be qualified to be in the ministry today if it weren't for several guys, that by God's grace, I've learned to walk beside over the years. And they're not afraid to correct me when I'm sliding this way or that way. So we all need battle buddies . . . . We need a guy who can help us come back to our senses when we're going one way or another off track."[1]

Joshua had no trouble being that man when the situation called for it. In fact, Achan was not the only time Joshua had to confront another man off the battlefield. He had to do it again in chapter 9 after learning that he had been "snookered" by the Gibeonites.

Joshua summoned them, and he said to them, "Why did you deceive us, saying, 'We are very far from you,' when you dwell among us? Now therefore you are cursed, and some of you shall never be anything but servants, cutters of wood and drawers of water for the house of my God." They answered Joshua, "Because it was told to your servants for a certainty that the LORD your God had commanded his servant Moses to give you all the land and to destroy all the inhabitants of the land from before you—so we feared greatly for our lives because of you and did this thing. And now, behold, we are in your hand. Whatever seems good and right in your sight to do to us, do it." So he did this to them and delivered them out of the hand of the people of Israel, and they did not kill them. But Joshua made them that day cutters of wood and drawers of water for the congregation and for the altar of the LORD, to this day, in the place that he should choose. (9:22–27)

Note a couple of things here. First, these lying Gibeonites took God's command to wipe out the inhabitants more seriously than Joshua and the Hebrews did (v. 24). Remember, when the Gibeonite emissaries first came into the camp with their slick story about being from very far away? Joshua and the leaders did not inquire of the Lord about it. Consequently, they made a bad decision. They made a covenant with these frauds. Now some might ask why Joshua and the leaders couldn't just declare that covenant null and void, since they entered it based on a lie. But these leaders rightly understood to break a covenant "sworn to them by the LORD, the God of Israel" (v. 19) would have brought shame on God's name and his honor. What was done was done, and they had to live with it.

Yet to his credit, Joshua didn't let the Gibeonites slide in light of their deception. He didn't let them off the hook for their bad behavior. No, he called them out. He confronted them.

Again, sometimes our battle buddies need to be confronted. Sometimes the iron of one man must clash with the iron of another. Sometimes hard questions must be asked, and straight statements must be made. Ideally, it needs to be done like Joshua did it—face to face. On a recent *Stand Courageous* podcast and again at a conference, Stu Weber gave a great example of a battle buddy calling him out when he was in his late twenties that changed his trajectory:

> I'll never forget one time we were taking our children to camp in the wilderness. His battle buddy John had horses and other animals, and they were carrying all the gear. We didn't have horses. And so my boys were walking, and you know boys, they get distracted. And I was pushing a little hard, like I was particularly prone to do as a younger man. And I got more than a little short with a couple of my boys that were goofing around and not making time on the trail to get to the destination. I was really unaware of it . . . but we got to the camp, we got it set up, and the girls were sitting around in what we call the kitchen, which is basically a tarp.
>
> We're into the deep of the wilderness. It's beautiful. John and I climb halfway up a little hill. We sit on a rock, and we're watching some elk feed down on the other side. It's just gorgeous. All is right with the world. I'm in heaven, and my friend turns to me and says, "My friend, I don't ever want to hear you talk to one of your boys that way again." It woke me up. I almost punched him and said, "They're *my* sons!" I

didn't because he was telling so much truth about my own soul and its condition at the time that I was just struck and humbled. So I saluted and I said, "You're right, my friend, thank you. I hope to never to talk to one of my boys that way again." It changed my way of fathering in just a moment with a battle buddy. Otherwise, I have lost the battle for my family.[2]

We all need a battle buddy like that in our lives who will shoot straight with us. And we need to be that sort of battle buddy for another man. Proverbs 27:17 shows how we can plug ourselves into such a friendship: "Iron sharpens iron, and one man sharpens another." This analogy was easily relatable to the average guy in ancient Israel. One piece of iron was used to sharpen another piece of iron until both became more effective tools or weapons. This commonplace visual aid of sharpening an implement of work or weapon of war provides us a practical model for the battle buddy relationship.

First, one man's life must *make and maintain contact with another man's life*. "Better is a neighbor who is near than a brother who is far away" (Prov. 27:10b). For sharpening to happen, the metals must be in close proximity, they must come together. The first negative statement in the Bible is about man being alone (see Gen. 2:18). Alone is not good. Left alone, both blades remain dull and useless. So it is with men. We are better together. Ecclesiastes 4:9–12 (NLT) nails this principle for us:

> Two people are better off than one, for they can help each other succeed. If one person falls, the other can reach out and help. But someone who falls alone is in real trouble. Likewise, two people lying close together can keep each other warm. But how can one be warm alone? A person standing alone can be attacked and

defeated, but two can stand back-to-back and conquer. Three are even better, for a triple-braided cord
is not easily broken.

Alone we are vulnerable. Together we can be unbeatable. We
must make and maintain contact with another man.

Second, battle buddies not only must maintain close contact,
but also *work in concert with one another.* You must stay in sync. It
takes focused cooperation to achieve the desired result. With iron,
the desired result is sharpness; with men, it is usefulness, effective-
ness, success. You don't simply "hang out" together and it magi-
cally happens. There must be purpose and direction to it. When
there is that intentionality, one man can be used by God to help
the other man become a better version of himself, and vice versa.
The implication is that the relationship is not only intentional, but
mutually beneficial. Both pieces of iron must be worked in concert and cooperation to accomplish the goal of sharpness.

Stu Weber explains the iron-sharpens-iron concept in the
lives of men and breaks it down in our Stand Courageous Conferences in four ways:

1. Acceptance

There's a powerful force that holds the iron against the iron.
That powerful force in a man's relationship or friendship we call
the powerful force of acceptance. You accept one another as
Christ accepted you, which means you didn't have to be totally
clean. You didn't have to be totally pure. He accepts you because
he loves you, and that's powerful. The force of acceptance will
keep you and grow you and make you more of the man God
intended you to be. Stu often shares a quote he picked up about
acceptance: "A friend is one who knows you as you are, under-
stands where you've been, accepts who you've become, and still
invites you to grow."

Stu then illustrates what it meant in his life:

> I had a coach when I was a sophomore in high school.
> I didn't know which way was up. I knew where the
> goal was, but I couldn't shoot to save my life. But this
> coach, he knew me. One day, I got seven rebounds
> in a game. You and I know seven's not all that much
> as a rebound, but I got seven. On the way out of the
> gym, he put his hand on my shoulder, slapped me
> on the butt, and he said, "You got seven rebounds.
> I bet you next week you get ten." That was affirma-
> tion, acceptance. "I got you for seven, I bet you grow."
> Next week, I got twelve. He said, "You got a dozen
> rebounds. Whoa, what a guy! Scrap, jump, fight
> every loose ball, yours. I accept you for who you are;
> you don't have to shoot. All your points are inside
> eight feet, but keep going the way you're going." It
> kept going to twenty-three rebounds because he
> accepted me for who I was. He didn't say to go out
> there and shoot and make a million points. He said
> to go out there and get all the loose balls. He accepted
> me for who I was, where I was, and he made a better
> player out of me.

That's what we're talking about, the power of acceptance,
holding the two pieces of iron together, men making and maintaining contact.

2. Affirmation

Second, there is that smoothing lubricant we call affirmation. You need some lubrication if you're going to work those
two pieces of metal together with the hopes of achieving a fine
edge on that blade. We call that lubrication in the masculine

friendship the power of affirmation. Psychologists tell us that being affirmed is one of the greatest needs of a man—we long for it. Have you ever tried to affirm yourself? What a losing battle that is. If we can affirm one another, we begin to build strength into one another. Stu compares his basketball coach's approach with that of his football coach:

> Along with the basketball coach, we also had a football coach who took the other approach. Instead of accepting and affirming, he beat you down. He took the same athletes and never had a great season like the basketball coach did. It wasn't because we were more basketball players than football players. It was because we had acceptance and affirmation, and we would have died for him.

Acceptance and affirmation must be there to achieve the desired result between two battle buddies. The next mission? Accountability.

3. Accountability

This is that word most men shy away from, which is understandable because it makes us uncomfortable. Without the lubrication, metal against metal causes friction. It creates heat. Sparks can fly. So it is when a man tries to hold another man accountable outside the context of a friendship based on acceptance and affirmation. Stu recounts:

> We had a kid in Ranger School. His name was Sanderson. He wasn't built to run. He had hips wider than his shoulders, and it was hard. We were on a platoon run. I don't know how many miles with full gear. It was several. You could see Sanderson's head start

to lull two rows in front of me, and I'll be darned if another Ranger didn't take his helmet so he didn't have to carry that steel pot. Another one took his rifle, and the words were, "Come on, Sanderson. You can do this. You're in First Platoon. We do this together while we're running." Sanderson finished the run. He would never have been qualified to make it given his physical prowess, but he had his brothers encouraging him and holding him accountable. "You're not dropping out, Sanderson. You're in First Platoon. You're with us. You keep running." And he did.

First acceptance and affirmation, and then accountability is better received. But accountability is critical. We need another man in our lives whom we allow to ask the hard questions, to "get in our grill" when we take a wrong turn, to call us out when we need it. There is another proverb from this same chapter that makes the point: "Better is open rebuke than hidden love. Faithful are the wounds of a friend; profuse are the kisses of an enemy" (Prov. 27:5–6).

Think about David's battle buddy Jonathan. What if Jonathan had lived and David never had to write that sad lament at the loss of his friend (see 2 Sam. 1:25–26)? When David lost Jonathan, he was never the same. If Jonathan had lived, there may never have been a "Bathsheba failure" in David's life. Perhaps Jonathan would have questioned David when he decided to stay home while the army went off to war. Maybe he would have stepped in and called out David when he issued the invitation to Bathsheba to come up to the palace. Maybe Jonathan would have pressed him when they were doing target practice, "The last two times we've been out here on the range you've mentioned that same married woman. You need to back off." Just think, if Jonathan had been around to hold David accountable, he might have saved David from that terrible sin, the lowest point of an otherwise exemplary life.

For those who know the details of David's life, the other low point was his relationship with his children. His son Amnon raped David's daughter Tamar. David's weak response? He got mad but did nothing according to 2 Samuel 13:21. In fact, the Dead Sea Scroll of this passage as well as the Greek Septuagint version of the Old Testament add: "But he would not punish his son Amnon, because he loved him, since he was his firstborn." Two years later, Absalom took revenge and killed Amnon, but David basically let him get away with it. Eventually, Absalom resented his father, attempted a coup, ran David off the throne, and died a tragic death. But what if Jonathan had been around to confront David when he failed to discipline his sons. Obviously, we will never know, but the point is this: we all need another man in our lives to whom we grant the permission and authority to hold us accountable. That brings us to the final point . . .

4. Authority

There's that really skillful angle that must be held to sharpen a blade that we call authority. To recap: first, we need the power that holds it together called acceptance. Second, we need that lubricant that keeps it working together in concert called affirmation. Next, we need the firm pressure of accountability, wearing off the rough and jagged down to the smooth. Finally, we need just the right angle to get that edge. The right angle must be maintained when the edge is pulled alongside the other metal to sharpen both. We must have the skill and timing to know just when to pull the trigger of authority to sharpen another man. Stu recounts how another man in his life showed such skill:

My sons got into high school competitive varsity athletics at the 6A level. The guys in the black and white shirts (referees) were messing with my boys, and [my temper] came out again, and I felt defeated. I was making a fool of myself in public. I started sermons on Sunday morning with public confession and apology for making a fool out of myself as a Christian believer in the middle of a pagan audience. It was terrible. What can I do? I couldn't win. My wife said, "Put on those earphones and move to the back of the crowd." It didn't work. I tried all those things.

Then I was in an accountability group. We thought it was a great thing back in the '90s. I drew two of the pastoral staff, one was the pastoral counselor. You know, counselors are nosey. They ask all kinds of questions. The other was the church administrator who by gifting is a nitpicker. And those sessions were difficult for me. But you know what? They became my friends, and that church administrator said, "If it would be helpful, I will go to those basketball games with you."

Now this is a guy who has five daughters. I have all boys. He never played basketball. He doesn't particularly relate to the game, and he came to the basketball games with me and sat beside me in the stands. When he could feel the temperature rise, all he did was put his hand on my knee . . . . What he said to me in a note was, "Stu, I know it's killing you. If it would be helpful to you, I'd be willing to go to the games with you. And when it comes at you, I'll be there with you." That is a battle buddy. He changed my life. He was the instrument that the Spirit of God used to bring that temper under control.

Stu granted his friend the authority to step in at just the right moment and help him become a better man. He concludes: "You and I need battle buddies if we're going to be what we're supposed to be as men." Acceptance, affirmation, accountability, and authority applied simultaneously by one battle buddy to the other will make both better men—iron sharpening iron.

Mentor Other Men –
Exodus 17; 24; 32–33; Numbers 27; Deuteronomy 31

If it isn't already obvious, Joshua is my (Boykin's) favorite biblical character. What an awesome responsibility was thrust on him when Moses informed him that he, Joshua, would lead the Israelites across the Jordan to conquer the promised land. For forty years Joshua walked in the footsteps of the great leader, Moses, expecting Moses to lead the conquest of Canaan. Suddenly Moses was telling Joshua the task was now his, because God was calling Moses home. The reason Joshua was ready for the mission was because he was mentored by Moses. Consequently, Moses is a model for every man who needs to find and mentor other men.

Remember, we first met Joshua when Moses chose him to lead the Israelite army in battle against the Amalekites in Exodus 17:8–13:

> Then Amalek came and fought with Israel at Rephidim. So Moses said to Joshua, "Choose for us men, and go out and fight with Amalek. Tomorrow I will stand on the top of the hill with the staff of God in my hand." So Joshua did as Moses told him, and fought with Amalek, while Moses, Aaron, and Hur went up to the top of the hill. Whenever Moses held up his hand, Israel prevailed, and whenever he lowered his hand, Amalek prevailed. But Moses' hands grew

weary, so they took a stone and put it under him, and he sat on it, while Aaron and Hur held up his hands, one on one side, and the other on the other side. So his hands were steady until the going down of the sun. And Joshua overwhelmed Amalek and his people with the sword.

One of the most important things you can do as a mentor is empower the man you are mentoring. Delegate responsibility to him. Let him know you trust him. While Moses made the major decisions, he allowed Joshua to make battlefield decisions. Moses showed Joshua he had confidence in him by trusting him with assuming command, selecting and organizing men for military service, and then leading this group of soldiers into battle as their field general. But Moses didn't throw Joshua in the deep end to let him sink or swim.

That reminds me of how I learned to swim. I loved my dad, but he was an old school Marine. He figured the best way for me to learn how to swim was to give me a ride on his shoulders as he waded out into the water and then dump me off in water over my head. When he got chest deep, that is exactly what he did. Man, it was literally sink or swim! Well, not really. My dad was within reach the whole time, cheering me on. I knew that if I went under, he would lift me out of that water. He would not let me drown. But you guessed it . . . I learned to swim that day.

Moses was there for Joshua when he led the armies of Israel into war against the Amalekites in his first military action. It was not sink or swim. While Moses was on the mountain watching the battle, he prayed for Joshua who was leading the troops in the valley. When Moses held high his staff, Joshua prevailed, but when Moses grew weary and his hands faltered, the momentum shifted and the Amalekites advanced. Yet in that critical moment, when victory or defeat hung in the balance, Aaron and Hur stepped in on either side of Moses to help him hold that staff high. God honored that symbolic action by giving prevailing strength to the Israelites, and Joshua triumphed over the enemy. From what we know, that was the beginning of the close, mentoring relationship between Moses and Joshua.

Don't miss the application: Are you praying for another man? Maybe you see a guy who is struggling, like Joshua did in that battle. When God puts another man on your heart, maybe because he seems to be losing the battle, pray for him. Bring him before the throne of God. Often one of the first steps in a mentoring relationship is prayer. Moses prayed for Joshua. As you survey the men in your world, is there one you especially feel compelled to bring to the Lord with sustained prayer?

From that moment forward, we see Moses intentionally developing Joshua as a leader. In the aftermath of that victory, we read: "Then the LORD said to Moses, 'Write this as a memorial in a book and recite it in the ears of Joshua, that I will utterly blot out the memory of Amalek from under heaven.' And Moses built an altar and called the name of it, The LORD Is My Banner, saying, 'A hand upon the throne of the LORD! The LORD will have war with Amalek from generation to generation'" (Exod. 17:14–16).

God saw Joshua as the future successor and wanted Moses to recite God's words "in the ears of Joshua." That is another function of a mentor—to communicate God's Word and wisdom to the man we seek to help grow and disciple. So here is the question: Are you having biblical conversations with another man? One way to do that is to plug into a Bible Reading Plan. Family Research Council takes a chronological approach as much as possible, reading the books of the Bible as they happen historically over two years. Visit FRC.org/Bible for the plan, and you can access daily questions from the readings you could forward to the man you are mentoring, as well as a weekly discussion guide for your time together around God's Word.

The words from God to be shared with Joshua after the victory over Amalek give us a preview of the next assignment Moses gave him. Joshua was privileged to accompany Moses up the mountain as his sole companion when Moses received the Ten Commandments from God at Sinai (Exod. 24:13). Joshua was given the opportunity to go places and see things even the seventy elders of Israel were not allowed to experience. One-on-one time with a mentor on a trip or a task is an important part of the discipleship process, especially if it is spiritually focused.

When the Israelites rebelled during their leaders' absence on the mountain, God told Moses and Joshua to make their way back down, and Joshua mistook their spiritual anarchy for warfare. Moses as mentor corrected that perspective quickly (Exod. 32:17–18), cluing Joshua in to what God had told him on the mountain. Later, Joshua would rebuke two men for prophesying in the camp, apparently jealous for his mentor, but Moses countered that it would please him if all the Lord's people became prophets (Num. 11:27–29). As a mentor, it is important to help course-correct mistaken perspectives, especially when it comes to belief and behavior, always pointing back to God's perspective as revealed in Scripture. In the end, Joshua observed Moses's righteous indignation when he smashed the two tablets of God's law in response to Israel's lewd worship of the golden calf (Exod. 32:19–20). He learned from his mentor that God will not tolerate any rivals and messing with God's holiness is serious business. The men we mentor should learn the same.

Following the severe judgment Moses meted out, we read that he brought Joshua to the Tent of Meeting, which was an earlier version of the tabernacle. There Joshua was privileged to witness the holy communion Moses had with the Lord as they spoke "face to face":

> Now Moses used to take the tent and pitch it outside
> the camp, far off from the camp, and he called it the
> tent of meeting. And everyone who sought the LORD
> would go out to the tent of meeting, which was out-
> side the camp. Whenever Moses went out to the tent,
> all the people would rise up, and each would stand
> at his tent door, and watch Moses until he had gone
> into the tent. When Moses entered the tent, the pillar
> of cloud would descend and stand at the entrance of
> the tent, and the LORD would speak with Moses. And
> when all the people saw the pillar of cloud standing
> at the entrance of the tent, all the people would rise
> up and worship, each at his tent door. Thus the LORD
> used to speak to Moses face to face, as a man speaks to
> his friend. When Moses turned again into the camp,
> his assistant Joshua the son of Nun, a young man,
> would not depart from the tent. (Exod. 33:7–11)

Don't miss what is said about Joshua in verse 11. Joshua
"would not depart from the tent." Many commentators deduce
that Joshua stood guard at the entrance to the Tent of Meeting. Yet guard duty is not given to generals. In fact, the original
Hebrew indicates that Joshua was not posted outside the tent,
but he was inside where God's presence appeared. And he didn't
leave. The text is literally rendered Joshua "departed not out of
the midst of the tent." Since Joshua as Moses's "assistant" or "servant" was also his understudy and ultimate successor, this additional time in the tent seems to have even greater significance.
Could it be that Joshua stayed behind because he was pursuing
intimacy with God like his mentor had? Surely, he heard the close
conversations between Moses and God. So it is not a stretch to
think that Joshua wanted time with God himself. Some might
consider this time with God necessary preparation for his future

leadership role, even though Joshua really didn't grasp all that God had in mind for him at that moment. Joshua was personally pursuing the Lord. Joshua was spending time in that tent because he wanted to worship the awesome and majestic God who had captured his heart. When you see the man whom you are mentoring wanting to spend more time passionately pursuing God, you know you are a successful mentor.

God's plan for Joshua unfolded further in the aftermath of Moses's prideful disobedience, forfeiting his privilege of entering the promised land. We've already considered Joshua's commission to lead the covert recon mission of the twelve "spies" behind enemy lines, and the way Joshua proved himself, as did Caleb, by demonstrating faith despite the fears of the majority. Consequently, only those two battle buddies would enter the land (Num. 13–14). That brings us to the next major development in Moses's mentoring relationship with Joshua in Numbers 27:

> Moses spoke to the LORD, saying, "Let the LORD, the God of the spirits of all flesh, appoint a man over the congregation who shall go out before them and come in before them, who shall lead them out and bring them in, that the congregation of the LORD may not be as sheep that have no shepherd." So the LORD said to Moses, "Take Joshua the son of Nun, a man in whom is the Spirit, and lay your hand on him." (Num. 27:15–18)

Once again, prayer is prominent when the time came for Moses's successor to be named. As a mentor, we need to be thinking ahead, have our eyes on the horizon, looking to the future. In humility, we must realize the day will come when our time is done, and another will take our place of leadership. We need to be preparing for that moment and praying for our successor.

Moses models that for us here. Pray in humility and sincerity and then expect God to answer.

God names the man Moses had mentored as his successor and his primary qualification: "Take Joshua the son of Nun, a man in whom is the Spirit, and lay your hand on him" (v. 18). Note that Joshua's intimacy with God comes to the forefront in this description. Joshua is a "man in whom is the Spirit." Obviously, God is speaking of the Holy Spirit. The Spirit of God empowered and directed his life. That ought to be the primary criterion by which we choose a leader. That time in the tent with God became evident.

Then God says, "Lay your hands on him." That's where we get the practice of ordination, symbolized by the laying on of hands, which goes all the way back to the sin offering in the law. A worshiper would come to the priest and offer a sin offering, and the priest would place his hands on that beast, and speak the sin of the worshiper, and then take the life of the beast, conferring the sin of that man on that beast. So God's command to lay on hands is symbolic of Moses conferring on Joshua the authority to lead. In fact, God spells that out in verse 20: "You shall invest him with some of your authority, that all the congregation of the people of Israel may obey." Great mentors share leadership with the men they are mentoring. Moses did that from this point all the way until the day he walked up that mountain and God took him home.

In verses 22–23, God basically tells Moses: "Let the people know that you support this man by laying hands on him publicly." So Joshua was to stand before Eliazar the priest and before the entire congregation as Moses led a public commissioning service. Moses did exactly as the Lord commanded. Moses did not have an ounce of self-pity or sour grapes in this whole deal—just obedience to God and support for Joshua. Great mentors publicly support and encourage the men they mentor.

One final thing Moses did for Joshua as his mentor was to bless his successor. In Deuteronomy 31, we read something of a renewal ceremony of this commissioning. Yet this time, Moses speaks an incredible word of blessing and challenge to Joshua: "Then Moses summoned Joshua and said to him in the sight of all Israel, 'Be strong and courageous, for you shall go with this people into the land that the Lord has sworn to their fathers to give them, and you shall put them in possession of it. It is the Lord who goes before you. He will be with you; he will not leave you or forsake you. Do not fear or be dismayed'" (Deut. 31:7–8).

What an encouragement that must have been for Joshua to hear these hope-filled words from his mentor. You can almost see it play out. Moses lays his hands upon Joshua's head. He speaks these words of commission and challenge into Joshua's ears and into his heart. Moses blesses him. A blessing is more than simply a word of affirmation. A blessing means more than a letter of recommendation. A blessing conveys a trust deeper than a mere handshake. A blessing breathes inspiration into the heart. A blessing pours confidence into the soul. A blessing speaks a word from God into the spirit. That's what Moses did for Joshua. That's what we need to do for other men.

As you read through the Scriptures, you see Moses investing into Joshua's life in a number of ways. Moses helped ensure the following generation would love and fear God by pouring his life into another who would lead them to do just that. Those forty years of following in the footsteps of Moses and being in the presence of God prepared Joshua for the greatest task of his life: bringing an end to the wilderness wandering and a new beginning in the promised land. And immediately after Moses's death, Joshua was ready to lead Israel to do all that God had commanded and promised.

Notably, Joshua succeeded in all points but one—he failed to mentor a successor as Moses had mentored him. Search the biblical record, and there is nothing to indicate that Joshua invested in a successor. There is nothing in Scripture to suggest that Joshua intentionally developed any future leaders. We don't read of him pouring into any individuals like Moses poured into him. As a result, when Joshua and his generation died, the Holy Spirit offers this sad epitaph in the Scriptures:

> And the people served the LORD all the days of Joshua, and all the days of the elders who outlived Joshua, who had seen all the great work that the LORD had done for Israel. . . . And all that generation also were gathered to their fathers. And there arose another generation after them who did not know the LORD or the work that he had done for Israel. And the people of Israel did what was evil in the sight of the LORD and served the Baals. And they abandoned the LORD, the God of their fathers, who had brought them out of the land of Egypt. They went after other gods, from among the gods of the peoples who were around them, and bowed down to them. And they provoked the LORD to anger. (Judg. 2:7, 10–12)

Joshua should have mentored another man to take his place, to lead Israel into the future under God. Because he didn't do what Moses did for him, the whole nation suffered. After Joshua's death, the generation that followed didn't even know the Lord. Israel drifted away from God, served the very idols of their enemies, and the result was chaos and defeat.

Let's bring it to our current day. Are *you* mentoring anyone? You should be, or you should at least be looking for that opportunity. There may be newcomers to the faith, or fatherless youth, or those who just need help dealing with their struggles. And please don't think because you've had setbacks or failures you can't be a mentor. That line of reasoning is deception from the enemy. All men have had failures of one kind or another.

We trust you'll pray for God to send you someone to mentor, or even for someone to mentor you. Mentoring is another way of being a battle buddy. Mentoring is a unique opportunity for us to share our own experiences—the good ones and the bad ones—in light of what God says in his Word, to provide wise counsel, to offer biblical encouragement, and to be a blessing to another man or even a young boy. We think it's something many men overlook. If Joshua did, it can happen to us too.

So how do we go about selecting someone to mentor? Dr. Stu Weber provided some seasoned wisdom on the topic at a recent Stand Courageous men's conference:[3]

Take It to the Lord: Begin by praying: "Lord, send me someone to mentor. Someone I can be completely honest with about all of my weaknesses and how I have learned from them, be totally humble with, pray with, pour into, and disciple." Our God is faithful. He knows how to give good gifts to his children, and he will answer.

Take Down the Names: Then write a list of men who God brings to your heart and mind. They don't know you well yet, but you know them well enough to appreciate them. Maybe you don't even know the guy's name, but you've noticed the guy always parks in a pickup over in a particular part of the church parking lot. And he comes in with his wife and young family, and he looks like somebody you'd like to know. Somehow you have been drawn to this guy or seen some potential in him from a distance. Introduce yourself, find out his name, and put the name on the list. Pray specifically about these men. Watch and listen to the Lord.

Take the Initiative: Once God begins to point to a particular candidate for mentoring, go ahead and take the initiative. Buy a men's book, like *Man to Man*. Get two copies, and give him one and keep one for yourself. Invite him to lunch and say: "Hey, here's a really good book I'm reading. How about reading the first chapter before we have lunch, and lunch is on me. If it is time well spent, we'll keep going. And if not, you've got a free lunch and a free book." And if you get turned down by a guy in the sovereignty of God, that's a good thing because he wasn't the one.

Take the Time: Finally, take the time to meet. I meet every week with other men, and we deliberately don't schedule appointments on the back side of it. We leave it open-ended. And sometimes it's an hour for breakfast, but often it's two and a half hours of worship and growth. We have no agenda except us before God, and it always turns into something powerful. Maybe you can't do that because of obligations, but take the time. Mentoring is an investment.

So you pray and take it before the Lord, you write down names and make the list, you take the initiative, you take the time to develop regular contact, and then you practice the forays of accepting and affirming and holding accountable and becoming authoritative. When you find that man who is humble and has an authentic awareness of his own needs, read a good book on biblical manhood and start having some honest conversations. Get real and confess to one another, talking about things that guys need to talk about; watch what happens. You can find those guys. They are out there. It works. It really works.

Here again is the soul-searching question: If you were to hand over your leadership assignment and pass the baton today, would there be someone who could take it and run with it?

Are you more like Moses or more like Joshua? Moses proactively and intentionally invested his life in Joshua. While Israel enjoyed great prosperity and victory under Joshua, he failed to invest in younger men who would lead the people of God into their future. We can't do anything about yesterday, but under God we can do something about tomorrow.

So let us rephrase the challenge: Will you be like Moses or like Joshua? Will you invest in others who will ensure that the generations to come will "know the LORD" and "the work that he had done for Israel" (Judg. 2:10)? Men, we must mentor other men. The future of our families, our churches, our communities, and our country depends on it. What are you waiting for? Start praying that God will point out your "Joshua" and get started!

BATTLE BUDDY GROUP GUIDE

Week 5 – Man as Mentor

▶ A Mentor Makes Himself Available
LTG (RET.) Jerry Boykin from his book *Man to Man*

Not long after I retired [from the Army], I was speaking at a men's conference in Richmond, Virginia, focusing my teaching about men becoming "Kingdom Warriors." At the end of that session, a man came up to me and said, "My name is Steve, and I'm with the Virginia State Police. I don't know why, but I feel like the Lord just told me to come up here and ask if you'd be willing to mentor me."

I'd never seen the man before. And I hadn't recently thought much about mentoring. But I answered right away, "Yeah, sure. I will."

And so began my mentoring relationship with Steve. I didn't see him often, but we kept in touch by phone and email. . . . He was a big, fit guy. And while serving as a state policeman, he came to Christ, and became a faithful Christian, although, like all of us, he was still learning. He volunteered to serve as a chaplain for the police, which meant he would officiate at funerals and fulfill a number of other responsibilities and obligations on a volunteer basis.

Before long, a new state police superintendent took charge. For some reason, he put out a decree saying something like, "You chaplains can no longer pray in the name of Jesus."

I first heard about that disturbing announcement on the news. Then a short time later while I was driving, I got to thinking about Steve. I knew he had to be struggling with that new edict. Right then, at that moment, I had the impulse to check on him. So I punched his number into my car phone.

When he answered, I said, "Steve, what are you doing?"

"So . . ." he began, "funny you should ask. I'm just getting ready to hit 'send' on an email to the superintendent. I'm gonna tell him that I'm not going to be a chaplain anymore."

That would have stopped me in my tracks if I hadn't been speeding in the fast lane.

"Steve, don't do that!" I told him. "Instead, go in and see the superintendent personally. That's the manly thing to do. Tell him to his face that if you can't pray according to your faith, that you respectfully resign. But don't burn any bridges other than by resigning."

Because of the mentoring relationship we shared, I believe the Lord laid Steve on my heart at the very moment he was about to press the "send" button. Instead, Steve erased the email, made an appointment, and soon went in to explain his situation to his new boss.

Had Steve put his situation in writing and sent it off in an email, it would have proliferated—there's no such thing as an email between only two people, especially if there's a controversy involved. In fact, even so, Steve's refusal to continue as a chaplain became a big story in the state of Virginia. The media managed to find a way to position Steve as the ringleader of a revolt against the new state police superintendent. Unsurprisingly, that's the way some journalists chose to categorize it.

As it turned out, some of the other chaplains followed suit. But again, if Steve had sent that initial email, it would have looked like there had been some kind of conspiracy, with similar emails stirring up other chaplains with the intention of launching a protest. So, to stop the story's momentum right then and there, I encouraged him to have another one-on-one conversation with the superintendent and leave it at that. . . .

He has since retired from the police force and is serving at Liberty University as the Director of Public Safety. But I'll always remember how God brought us together and I became a mentor to him. In the ten years we've had a mentoring relationship, our relationship has become close and meaningful. The Holy Spirit will often prompt me to call this man, and it always turns out to be at a moment when he is in a battle of some kind. And he's also there when I need him with wise counsel. We always discuss the situation and then we pray.

Thankfully, he is still doing very well. . . .

What made Steve want me to be his mentor? First of all, he had the strong impression that God was specifically leading him to ask me if I'd be willing take on that role. Also, his career in law enforcement probably caused him to look for someone who could understand his responsibilities and his role, which occasionally required violence and physical confrontation. My military background, and perhaps something he'd heard me say, led him to want my guidance in his life. And I had the strong impression that it would be good for us both if I could provide it.[4] ◄

Group Debrief

Mentoring is important but often neglected. Maybe it is because the whole concept of opening ourselves up and being transparent makes us uncomfortable. Whatever the reason, the need is great. The apostle Paul told Timothy, whom he was mentoring to become a church leader: "You, therefore, my son, be strong in the grace that is in Christ Jesus. What you have heard from me in the presence of many witnesses, commit to faithful men who will be able to teach others also" (2 Tim. 2:1–2 CSB).

While we may not be on the level of an apostle Paul developing the likes of a Timothy for pastoral ministry, or Moses developing Joshua for leading a nation, we should aspire to mentor someone just like General Boykin mentored Steve. Or like Steve, find someone who can mentor us.

Questions to Consider

- Have you been mentored, formally or informally? If not, do you think you might need a mentor? Pray about who might become a mentor to you.

- Have you ever tried to mentor another guy? If so, describe how you went about it? What worked well?

- If you have not mentored someone, what are the biggest reasons holding you back?

- Is there someone God may be calling you to mentor? Commit the matter to prayer then follow through on God's prompting.

CHAPTER 6
Man as a Chaplain

In the opening pages of Genesis, we get a clear picture that God delegated to Adam responsibility for the spiritual well-being of his wife, and later, his family. While all the biblical roles are vital, the role of chaplain is perhaps most important. Tony Perkins, President of Family Research Council, argues this point well in our Stand Courageous Conferences:

> Biblical masculinity calls men and prepares men to be the Provider, the Defender, the Mentor, and the Instructor in their home. But the foundational role of the biblical man is that of Chaplain, the spiritual leader of their home: the one who educates, exhorts, and provides an earnest example of how to stand courageously for the Lord in every situation . . . . Simply put, no father, no family, no faith.[1]

Consequently, our goal is for every man, husband, and father to become an active spiritual leader, first of all in his own home. For that to happen, there must be a vital love relationship with God, an intimate knowledge of his Word, and an intentional plan to impart Bible truth to those in your charge. Moses directed this instruction to parents:

> "Listen, Israel: The LORD our God, the LORD is one. Love the LORD your God with all your heart, with all your soul, and with all your strength. These words that I am giving you today are to be in your heart. Repeat them to your children. Talk about them when you sit in your house and when you walk along the road, when you lie down and when you get up. Bind them as a sign on your hand and let them be a symbol on your forehead. Write them on the doorposts of your house and on your city gates." (Deut. 6:4–9 CSB)

Note the order. First, love God with every fiber of your being. Second, put his Word in your heart (which is a sign of the first). Third, plan to pass on his Word and the practice of prayer to your family. In addition to having your own personal walk with God and a plan to communicate spiritual truth to those in your charge, you must also call them to commitment as Joshua did with his final words. This is the role and responsibility of chaplain that God has delegated to us as men. Now allow me to add a thought here. Some men think that because of their past failures, they are being hypocritical with their children or wife when they advocate for a life of obedience and love for Christ. They feel unworthy. The reality is that if you have confessed those sins, they are forgotten according to 1 John 1:9. So what you are also doing is demonstrating God's grace and love, which brings his forgiveness to all who seek it.

Face to Face – Joshua 5:13–15

Have you ever thought you were alone, only to find out you were not? I (Cureton) was fly fishing in Pacific Creek in Grand Teton National Park, landing a couple of nice Snake River Cutthroats, when I sensed something was over to my right in the willows that stretched up over my head. Then I smelled it. Suddenly I knew

I was not alone. Then I saw it. A baby moose parted the thick willows. Those critters are so ugly they are cute, but seeing that little one was not my concern. My question at that moment was: "Where is mama?" Mother moose are particularly defensive of their young and have been known to kill people. Park personnel will tell you more people are killed by moose than bears.

Sure enough, big mama's nose parted the willows behind her little one, and she took two steps forward as I took three steps back. She took one look at me and made a guttural sound, and I was close enough to see the hair on her neck stand up straight. Any second she could charge and trample me, so that was my cue to exit. So I slowly backed away into the willows and headed upstream. Thinking I was a safe distance away, I started to cast. But before I could get my fly back on the water, I had that same feeling I was not alone. There was something big just up ahead in the willows. Again, I smelled it before I saw it. This time it was a massive lone buffalo, munching his way toward me. Time to find a new fishing hole!

Back in Joshua chapter 5, we read that Joshua also suddenly sensed that he was not alone. Rewind in our study and remember, this is before Jericho fell. At this point, Joshua was still pondering that impossible-looking situation. He looked up at those massive walls and he probably thought, *It just can't be done!* When was the last time you went out to look at the problems facing you, your family, your community? Maybe you've sized up the situation and shook your head and said, "There's no way." Well, that's exactly what Joshua was doing when he became aware of another presence in verses 13–15:

> When Joshua was near Jericho, he looked up and saw
> a man standing in front of him with a drawn sword
> in his hand. Joshua approached him and asked, "Are
> you for us or for our enemies?" "Neither," he replied.

"I have now come as commander of the LORD's army."
Then Joshua bowed with his face to the ground in
worship and asked him, "What does my lord want
to say to his servant?" The commander of the LORD's
army said to Joshua, "Remove the sandals from your
feet, for the place where you are standing is holy."
And Joshua did so.

Imagine Joshua picking his way down a path, watching
where he's putting his feet, and then suddenly sensing that he
is not alone. He stops, slowly lifts his eyes, and sees a man with
a drawn sword in his hand. His breathing increases, adrenaline
rushes, heart races, and instinctively, he reaches for his sword at
his side ready for a fight. But he pauses to ask, "Are you a friend
or a foe? Are you for us or against us? Are you on our side or on
their side?" Joshua receives a strange answer: "Neither." Essentially this mysterious heavenly being is saying, "I'm not on your
side or their side; I've not come to take sides; I've come to take
over!"

Listen, if you want victory in your life, stop trying to get
God on your side. Get on God's side! Stop trying to get him to
bless your mess. Hit the restart with him in the lead. You will
never know victory, and your Jericho will never fall, until you
do as Joshua did and lay your sword down and bow down before
God. Then your problem is no longer yours; it becomes God's
problem—and for God it is no problem at all. That makes all
the difference in the world, doesn't it? See, Joshua had been
problem-conscious, and now he became God-conscious. He's
lying flat on his face on the ground before this angelic messen-
ger, and Joshua's no longer thinking about why it can't be done.
He realizes that it *will* be done, because God has got this!

There are a lot of men who just look at the challenges, the
problems, the impossibilities, all the reasons why it can't be

done. We all experience this from time to time. Yet if we want our Jericho to fall, we've got to look past our problems and lock onto the Lord Jesus Christ, who is the Captain of our faith.

So Joshua laid his sword at the feet of the captain of the Lord's heavenly hosts and bowed down in reverence. And this supernatural commander said, "Remove the sandals from your feet, for the place where you are standing is holy ground." And Joshua took off his sandals. Remember that happening before? Right, it happened at the burning bush. God spoke to Moses these same words in Exodus 3:5. Joshua was dealing with the "Angel of Presence," who represented the God of Angel Armies.

Do you want to conquer your circumstances? Do you want to be a victorious man like Joshua? If you want to be a conqueror, you must first be conquered. Has that happened to you? Have you bowed before him in submission? Have you given everything to Jesus Christ? If you haven't, no wonder your Jericho is still there. Submit yourself to the Captain of the heavenly hosts. This does not mean you are not expected to take action yourself, but you are to trust the Lord to guide you in your actions to be victorious.

If you want to become the spiritual leader of your home—the chaplain, the priest of the group God has entrusted to you—you must have a life-changing encounter with God. If you have not already, you need to bow before Jesus as Lord, turn from your sin, put your trust in him, then surrender to him as Lord. When that happens, everything will begin to change (2 Cor. 5:17). As you "taste and see that the LORD is good" (Ps. 34:8), you won't dread meeting with God; it will become your desire. King David wrote:

> God, you are my God; I eagerly seek you. I thirst
> for you; my body faints for you in a land that is dry,
> desolate, and without water. So I gaze on you in the

sanctuary to see your strength and your glory. My lips will glorify you because your faithful love is better than life. So I will bless you as long as I live; at your name, I will lift up my hands. You satisfy me as with rich food; my mouth will praise you with joyful lips. When I think of you as I lie on my bed, I meditate on you during the night watches because you are my helper; I will rejoice in the shadow of your wings. I follow close to you; your right hand holds on to me. (Ps. 63:1–8)

Like David, we pray you will begin to look forward to spending time with the God who made you, who loves you, who sent Jesus to die for you, who wants you to be with him forever. To cultivate that relationship, you must talk with God and walk with God and meet with God. There are no substitutes or shortcuts to this. Obviously, this God-meeting Joshua just had was unexpected, and that will happen from time to time. However, your meetings should be planned. They need to happen daily. Put a reminder in your phone. We have a couple of daily Bible reading plans at the back of this resource. Meet God in his Word. Listen for his voice in its pages. Meditate on what he is saying to you in the verses you read. Write it down. Keep a journal.

During your time, talk to God. Begin by praising him for who he is and thanking him for what he does. Begin to count your blessings as you approach God. Ask for his help aligning your character, habits, and decisions with his Kingdom agenda and revealed will in Scripture. Talk with him about the needs and challenges you have today. Pray for those in your care by name and specific need. Ask him to point out sins you have committed (or commands not obeyed) and for his forgiveness and a fresh start. Also ask for help forgiving those who have wronged you.

Call on his assistance to stay out of Satan's snares and that he would keep you off the path toward temptation and on the path to living a life that pleases him. Finally, acknowledge him as your God and give him glory. Sound familiar? It should. That's basically the way Jesus taught his disciples to pray in what we call the Lord's Prayer (Matt. 6:9–13).

God has given you way too much responsibility to try to go it on your own without his equipping and empowering from his Word and time in prayer. During the Civil War, with casualties climbing and no end in sight, President Abraham Lincoln reportedly said: "I have been driven many times upon my knees by the overwhelming conviction that I had nowhere else to go. My own wisdom and that of all about me seemed insufficient."[2] If that was true for Lincoln, it is true for you as a leader, no matter the challenge.

Speaking of spending time on your knees, that was certainly true of the father of our country, George Washington. We have all seen the iconic image of General Washington kneeling in the snows of Valley Forge, praying to God. He was seen like that on numerous occasions, not only in the field, but also at home. In fact, his whole life through, whether he was a young man, an officer, a general, or the President of the United States, unless there was some absolute emergency that claimed his immediate attention, he spent time in the Bible and in prayer both morning and evening. On several occasions, different people who happened to be in the home, because of certain pressing matters that came up, felt compelled to interrupt Washington in his library. Often, they found him on his knees, in front of a chair with a candle on the stand next to the chair, and the Bible open before him, praying.[3] His adopted daughter, Nelly Parke Custis (Martha's granddaughter), did not spy on Washington's private devotions at Mount Vernon, but affirmed what others had witnessed:

It was his custom to retire to his library at nine or ten o'clock where he remained an hour before he went to his chamber. He always rose before the sun and remained in his library until called to breakfast. I never witnessed his private devotions. I never inquired about them. I should have thought it the greatest heresy to doubt his firm belief in Christianity. His life, his writings, prove that he was a Christian. He was not one of those who act or pray, "that they may be seen of men." He communed with his God in secret [see Matt. 6:5–6].[4]

For Washington, spending time alone with God in prayer before an open Bible was a persistent habit, thus it was a vital part of his everyday life. Certainly, God honored this man and heard his prayers.

An amazing thing happens when you begin meeting with God on a regular basis. If you do it with an open heart and a willing spirit, you'll find that eventually it will not be something you have to schedule; it will be something you long for. Something you cherish. Those times with God will become the best moments of your day! And those moments with God will create a reservoir you draw from as you impart spiritual guidance to those God has placed in your charge as the chaplain.

Daily Devotion – Joshua 8:30–35

The daily routine. We all have them. Morning rituals of getting ready for work. Hopefully, spending some meaningful time with God is one of them. Your family needs you to take the lead and show the way when it comes to a daily devotion—moments spent in God's Word and in worship. With the schedules we keep today, this is a tall order. But it is not impossible. It is just like everything else. You have to value it enough to make the effort and gather your family and engage them in a Bible-centered conversation.

For our (Cureton's) family, when our kids were young, it was at bedtime. We did a Bible story followed by prayer and singing a hymn. My kids still remember us singing "Amazing Grace" at bedtime. When they became school age, we also did some devotional time at the dinner table, reading the Bible and always a prayer. And yes, we had football, soccer, and band practice, piano and dance recital, etc. going on, but we made it happen as much as possible.

We invite you to take your family through the Stand on the Word Bible Reading Plan. The plan provides daily readings from the Bible chronologically over two years. In other words, each reading takes you through the Bible as events happen in history as far as it is possible. When you sign up, we provide you with a couple of suggested questions for each day that you can ask at breakfast, over the dinner table in the evening, or you can send each morning via text to your family. Then there is a weekly debrief to use on Sundays for a time of Bible-centered discussion. Visit frc.org/Bible to get started or text the word "Bible" to 67742. Also, we do a weekly devotion for men from the Bible readings that can be found at StandCourageous.com.

As we read Joshua 8 in the aftermath of their victory at Ai, we find that Joshua took time away from the battlefield to lead Israel into the presence of the Lord to renew the covenant with him. Now that probably seems strange from a strategic perspective. Most observers likely would have counseled the continuation of the military campaign. Capture and control the central section of the land—the hill country. Why not finish off the enemy now? It is called "Exploiting a Success" in modern military terms. But Joshua, sensitive to God's timing, instead led the people on a pilgrimage to meet with the Lord at a predetermined location. In fact, Moses had given specific directions for this before he died

(Deut. 27:1–8). As you read what Joshua did with the family of Israel, think of applications to the spiritual leadership of your family.

> At that time Joshua built an altar to the Lord, the God of Israel, on Mount Ebal, just as Moses the servant of the Lord had commanded the people of Israel, as it is written in the Book of the Law of Moses, "an altar of uncut stones, upon which no man has wielded an iron tool." And they offered on it burnt offerings to the Lord and sacrificed peace offerings. And there, in the presence of the people of Israel, he wrote on the stones a copy of the law of Moses, which he had written. And all Israel, sojourner as well as native born, with their elders and officers and their judges, stood on opposite sides of the ark before the Levitical priests who carried the ark of the covenant of the Lord, half of them in front of Mount Gerizim and half of them in front of Mount Ebal, just as Moses the servant of the Lord had commanded at the first, to bless the people of Israel. And afterward he read all the words of the law, the blessing and the curse, according to all that is written in the Book of the Law. There was not a word of all that Moses commanded that Joshua did not read before all the assembly of Israel, and the women, and the little ones, and the sojourners who lived among them. (8:30–35)

Again, this episode from the life of Joshua illustrates what it means to be the spiritual leader. Joshua built the altar. Joshua copied the Law of Moses onto several stones. Joshua read the Word of God to the men and the women, even to the little ones and the guests. He set the pace and established the priority of honoring God's Word.

Many Christians often experience defeat in their walk because they fail to spend time with the Lord before an open Bible, hear from him, thank him and praise him, and put on their spiritual armor to face that day's battles. Our capacity for overcoming difficulties in life has a direct correlation to our investment in pursuing a relationship with God. In Jeremiah 29:13, God instructs us: "You will seek me and find me when you seek me with all your heart." Guys, we need to be seeking the Lord with all our hearts.

This pursuit was no small thing for Joshua and the people of Israel. After the victory over Ai, the whole nation of men, women, children, and livestock moved from their base camp at Gilgal, northward up the Jordan Valley to the place designated by Moses between Mount Ebal (v. 30) and Mount Gerizim (v. 33), which are at Shechem. This would have been a journey of over twenty miles. The point is, it takes effort; it takes an investment to meet with God. Plus, it was a priority. This spiritual pursuit took precedence over the continuation of the military campaign in which they were engaged. It is the same for us. If we are to succeed in our mission as chaplains and spiritual leaders, it has to be a priority and it will necessitate effort and investment.

Why was Shechem chosen as the location? From a practical perspective, this area between the mountains created a natural amphitheater for such a large number of people. Apparently, this place has outstanding acoustical properties so that people standing on one mountain could be heard by those standing on the other mountain. From a strategic perspective, these mountains are located near the geographic center of the land. Shechem became the central meeting place.

More important than its centrality, this location had serious spiritual significance. Abram stopped at the tree of Moreh
in Shechem. There God confirmed his promise to give the land
to him, and Abram built an altar at the site (Gen. 12:7). Jacob,
Abram's grandson, also built an altar at Shechem, calling it "El
Elohe Israel," meaning "mighty God of Israel" (Gen. 33:18–20).
And the remains of Jacob's son Joseph were buried at Shechem
(Josh. 24:32). So the altar at Shechem was recognized as a sanctuary of the Lord (24:26). Indeed, Shechem was a worship center
from this time to when Joshua gave his farewell address (cf. 24:1)
and for some 400 years. It is here that Joshua led the people to
renew the covenant with God.

That raises a question: Do you have a place that you and
your family regularly meet with God? Are you a part of a Bible-
centered church? Part of your mission as a chaplain is to lead
your family in participation and partnership in a place of worship, a local body of believers. Bear in mind, our role as a chaplain is broader than just within the family, but the focus here is
on our role as the chaplain in the home.

Now Moses had already instructed them about what to do
there in Deuteronomy 27:12–14: "When you have crossed over
the Jordan, these shall stand on Mount Gerizim to bless the
people: Simeon, Levi, Judah, Issachar, Joseph, and Benjamin.
And these shall stand on Mount Ebal for the curse: Reuben,
Gad, Asher, Zebulun, Dan, and Naphtali. And the Levites shall
declare to all the men of Israel in a loud voice . . . ."

The blessings and the curses from the law were to be read,
and the people were to respond with "Amen!" So Mount Ebal
stood for cursing, and Mount Gerizim stood for blessing.

Consequently, this event between the two mountains formed
a huge object lesson. What happened to the Israelites in the land,
the history of Israel, was going to depend on where they "lived."
Would they live on Mount Ebal, in disobedience and under the

curses? Or would they live on Mount Gerizim, in obedience and under God's blessing? As we encourage our family in the Word of God, it is always helpful to remind them that our choices have consequences—blessings if we obey and curses if we disobey. The covenant renewal ceremony Joshua led had three parts that followed Moses's instruction in Deuteronomy 27 and has much to teach us about our role as chaplains.

1. The Sacrifice

Sacrifices were made to the Lord on an altar made of uncut stones—burnt offerings and peace offerings in accordance with the Law of God (Josh. 8:30–31; see Lev. 1, 3). Israel now publicly renewed the covenant originally made at Sinai. However, that generation, with the notable exception of Joshua and Caleb, was all dead and gone, victims of God's judgment in the wilderness because of their unbelief. Now a whole new generation swore allegiance to the one true God. Note three important principles:

First, this command to build an altar for sacrifice points to God's grace and solution for sin. Why make these sacrifices? Because we all fall short when it comes to our obedience to the Law. In fact, the same was true back when they made a covenant with God at Sinai. Right after God gave the Ten Commandments, he also instituted the sacrifices. At the same time, he gave them Moses and Aaron the high priest. It was as if God were saying, "Thou shalt not . . . , but I know you will, and here is your way to escape judgment through an atoning sacrifice." So Joshua did as Moses commanded and built an altar.

Second, the altar was to be built on Mount Ebal, the place where the curses for disobedience were to be read. Why this place instead of the place that represented blessing for obedience? Obviously, because the altar on Mount Ebal was for sinners. God knew they would break his law, but he graciously made provision for it on the very mountain where the curses were pronounced. We need to teach our families that we need to come clean and confess our sins so we can access God's gracious provision through Christ's atoning sacrifice. One of the most freeing verses in the Bible is 1 John 1:9: "If we confess our sins, he is faithful and just to forgive us our sins and to cleanse us from all unrighteousness." So the altar on Mount Ebal was for those who confess their sin and who would come not as self-righteous, but as sinners to the place of sacrifice to escape the curse.

Remember that conversation Jesus had with the Samaritan woman at the well in John 4? Interestingly, the Samaritans built an altar on Mount Gerizim, not Ebal. The choice of Gerizim for the altar suggests they came to God not as sinners but in their self-righteousness (see John 4:20). But Jesus exposed their spiritual ignorance, "You worship what you do not know . . ." (v. 22), and uncovered her sin: "you have had five husbands, and the one you now have is not your husband" (v. 18).

Third, the altar was constructed of uncut stones. In other words, there was no human workmanship involved—no hammer or chisel work. No improvements were made by man. What is the message? These uncut stones represent a complete negation and rejection of salvation by works. It shows we can add nothing to the work of God. When Jesus shouted: "It is finished" on the cross, that means his sacrifice for sin is complete and sufficient. We have nothing we can add by way of improvement. Consequently, as Paul put it: "For by grace you have been saved through faith. And this is not your own doing; it is the gift of God, not a result of works, so that no one may boast" (Eph. 2:8–9).

As we lead our families and even our friends and acquaintances through devotional times, we should remind them that:

- We must recognize our sinfulness and come to God as sinners (Rom. 3:23).

- We must come to the place of sacrifice, the cross, acknowledging our need of Christ to die in our place (Rom. 5:8).
- We must reject any human effort for salvation and recognize there is nothing we can do or add to the work of God's substitute for our sin on that cross (Eph. 2:8–9).

To recap, Joshua sacrificed on the altar made of uncut stones. Now let's look at what he did with another set of stones mentioned in verse 32.

2. The Scriptures

On Mount Ebal, Joshua set up these large stones, plastered to make a smooth surface, and on their surface, he inscribed a copy of the Law of Moses. How much of the Law was inscribed is not precisely identified in the text. Some suggest only the Ten Commandments were written on these stones. Others think the stone inscriptions included the contents of at least part or all of Deuteronomy, the "second giving of the Law." In the ancient Near East, it was not uncommon for various cultures to inscribe lengthy writings in stone. In fact, archaeologists have discovered similarly inscribed pillars (or stelae) some six to eight feet long. Interestingly, the Behistun Inscription in Iran is nearly three times the length of Deuteronomy. So, it is entirely conceivable the whole contents of the Law were inscribed on these large stones, and the text indicates that was indeed the case.

Don't miss the fact that Joshua painstakingly inscribed the entire book of the Law of God in stone. That was a monumental task in and of itself. For something to be written in stone speaks of its importance, its permanence, and its centrality. Even if we were to take pen and paper, it would take quite some time to copy down the entire book of Deuteronomy. Yet this labor-intensive task points out just how important God's Word was to Joshua as their spiritual leader. He wanted to preserve God's Word because he revered it. He honored it. He was simply respecting what God told him all the way back in the first chapter. God said if you want to be a success, if you want to experience victory . . .

> "Only be strong and very courageous, being careful to do according to all the law that Moses my servant commanded you. Do not turn from it to the right hand or to the left, that you may have good success wherever you go. This Book of the Law shall not depart from your mouth, but you shall meditate on it day and night, so that you may be careful to do according to all that is written in it. For then you will make your way prosperous, and then you will have good success." (Josh. 1:7–8)

Yet Joshua is not copying down the Word of God on stone just for himself, but for posterity, all the future generations to come. Men, we must instill a reverence and honor for the Word of God in our families, as well as demonstrate a profound respect for God's Word to those in our circle of friends and associates. It starts with how we treat it ourselves. In fact, Moses laid out this challenge for fathers, beginning with what the Jewish people call the Shema in Deuteronomy 6:4–9:

> "Hear, O Israel: The LORD our God, the LORD is one. You shall love the LORD your God with all your heart and with all your soul and with all your might. And these words that I command you today shall be on your heart. You shall teach them diligently to your children, and shall talk of them when you sit in your house, and when you walk by the way, and when you lie down, and when you rise. You shall bind them as

a sign on your hand, and they shall be as frontlets between your eyes. You shall write them on the doorposts of your house and on your gates."

Notice the Word of God is to be on our hearts, and then we are to teach God's Word to our children. And there's no bad place to do it: at home or on the go. There's no bad time to do it: bedtime or first thing in the morning when they get up. Anytime and anyplace is fair game. Interestingly, that phrase "teach them diligently" translates a single Hebrew word that literally means to sharpen. It carries with it the picture of a sharp object that pierces or makes a penetrating mark on something else. Our biblical conversations are to penetrate the hearts of our sons and daughters and leave a lasting impression. We are to impact our children deeply with the Word of God. We are to imprint and inscribe these commandments on their hearts, similar to how Joshua inscribed the words into stone. That leads us to the third thing Joshua did.

3. The Sermon

When Joshua finished inscribing these stones with God's Word, he then led Israel in the renewal of the covenant at Shechem, between Mount Gerizim and Mount Ebal, by verbally reading it in their hearing. Joshua "read all the words of the law. . . . There was not a word of all that Moses commanded that Joshua did not read before all the assembly of Israel" (8:34–35). Joshua read through the entire book of Deuteronomy, which contains "the blessing and the curse" we read about in verse 34. Deuteronomy is more or less a collection of the sermons Moses preached before his death, restating the Law for a new generation of Israelites. In the audience listening to Joshua as he read these sermons was every member of the tribes of Israel: men, women, children, and even some "sojourners" or non-natives.

The hearing of the Law of God was so crucial to their future success as the people of God in this promised land.

Half of the people were positioned on the slopes of Mount Gerizim to the south; the other half were on the slopes of Mount Ebal to the north, and the ark of the covenant surrounded by priests was in the valley between. As the curses of the Law were read aloud one by one, the tribes on Mount Ebal responded, "Amen!" As the blessings were also read aloud, the tribes on Mount Gerizim responded "Amen!" (Deut. 11:29; 27:12–26). The huge natural amphitheater, which can be seen even to this day, made it possible for the people to hear every word, and the children of Israel affirmed that the Law of the Lord was indeed to be the law of the land.

The Law pointed the nation to those righteous statutes that would enable Israel to be a holy nation, a special redeemed people, a people of God's own possession and a light to the nations (see Exod. 19:4–6; Deut. 4:1–8). The Law pointed Israel and all men to those moral statutes that are so vital to justice and law and order within nations. But it did more. It demonstrated the holiness of God, and by virtue of man's inability to keep the Law, it showed man his sin, which separates him from God. The tabernacle, the sacrifices, and the priesthood pointed forward to a suffering Savior, the Lamb of God, who had to die for the sins of the world. That once-for-all sacrifice made reconciliation possible with God, so we can be adopted into his family as sons and daughters, the family of God in a fallen world. These are things we need to stress as we read through the Bible and pray as a family.

We also need to be warned by what happens when we don't take the time to do these daily devotions in God's Word and spend time in prayer with our families. Notice how quickly Israel's commitment to God faded from their minds, for in the very next book of the Bible, Judges, we read: "And there arose another generation after them who did not know the Lord or the work that he had done for Israel" (Judg. 2:10). Then we read the results near the end of the book: "In those days there was no king in Israel. Everyone did what was right in his own eyes" (Judg. 21:25).

We are no different today in America. Though our nation was founded on biblical principles, the moral Law of God, we have basically turned away from the Bible to do what is right in our own eyes. Because we have rejected God's Word and its application to every area of life, God is allowing us to sow the wind and reap the whirlwind. Romans 1 is being played out in our culture: "For although they knew God, they did not honor him as God or give thanks to him, but they became futile in their thinking, and their foolish hearts were darkened. Claiming to be wise, they became fools" (Rom. 1:21–22). As a result, God has given us up to all sorts of perversions and depravity (Rom. 1:23–32).

Bottom line: we are in desperate need of a moral revival, spiritual awakening, and a return to our biblical foundations as laid by our wise forefathers. The moral breakdown in society and in our leadership, especially for a nation with such godly beginnings, is almost beyond imagination. We are too much like Israel in this regard. Frankly, the survival of America depends on our willingness to repent and submit again to God and to the absolutes of his Word. And Christians must lead the way. Guys, we need to start in our own homes.

Consider the fact that if you were to worship together as a family at home each day, by the time your child was age eighteen, you would have had over 6,500 opportunities to read the Scriptures, pray and sing with him or her. If you read roughly a chapter from the Bible every day for eighteen years, you would read the Bible through five-and-a-half times. Think of the positive, cumulative effect on a child or grandchild of simply reading a chapter a day from the Bible.

So here is the question: Do you spend more time tending to your children's temporal needs than their spiritual needs? Are you more concerned about how well they do in school, perform in sports and other pursuits, the social group they run with, their success in secular employment, etc., than you are about their relationship with the Lord and their spiritual growth and maturity? Cyprian, renowned North African churchman of the third century, reportedly said that a father who is more concerned about the temporal needs than the spiritual needs of his kids was like a man watching his dog and his child drowning at the same time—but choosing to save his dog.[5] What a wake-up call! It is vital we take time daily to invest in the spiritual needs of our families, especially our children and grandchildren. Men, that is a major part of our mission as the chaplain.

Call to Commitment – Joshua 24:14–30

The book of Joshua contains an amazing story of the activity of God working through his people and their leader. We've seen a swollen river open up, massive walls fall down, and fierce giants taken out. Additionally, this book is an illustration of the victorious life of a "Strong and Courageous" Christian. For the Bible says: "All these things happened to them as examples for us" (1 Cor. 10:11). So, this book is more than a lesson in ancient Hebrew history; it teaches us we can be "more than conquerors through him who loved us" (Rom. 8:37). We can overcome difficulty, hardship, and opposition. We can walk in victory and lead our families to do the same as we wholeheartedly follow the Lord. Joshua, "God's General," models that for us like few others in the Scriptures.

As we come to the end of our journey with Joshua, there's one last episode in his life that commands our attention. Seeing his days on earth were few, Joshua called all Israel together at Shechem to challenge them to renew the covenant, call them to commitment, and confirm their willingness to serve the Lord; then he leads the way. Joshua gives this farewell address in chapters 23–24. Here's the first part:

> A long time after the LORD had given Israel rest from all the enemies around them, Joshua was old, advanced in age. So Joshua summoned all Israel, including its elders, leaders, judges, and officers, and said to them, "I am old, advanced in age, and you have seen for yourselves everything the LORD your God did to all these nations on your account, because it was the LORD your God who was fighting for you. See, I have allotted these remaining nations to you as an inheritance for your tribes, including all the nations I have destroyed, from the Jordan westward to the Mediterranean Sea. The LORD your God will force them back on your account and drive them out before you so that you can take possession of their land, as the LORD your God promised you.
>
> "Be very strong and continue obeying all that is written in the book of the law of Moses, so that you do not turn from it to the right or left and so that you do not associate with these nations remaining among you. Do not call on the names of their gods or make an oath to them; do not serve them or bow in worship to them. Instead, be loyal to the LORD your God, as you have been to this day. The LORD has driven out great and powerful nations before you, and no one is able to stand against you to this day. One of you routed a thousand because the LORD your God was fighting for you, as he promised. So diligently watch yourselves! Love the LORD your God!" (23:1–11 CSB)

By the time we get to the farewell address of Joshua, the children of Israel had nearly conquered the land. Yes, there were still battles to fight, areas of resistance to be rooted out, but they had the military situation well in hand. They were beginning the process of possessing the land as their own. Joshua wanted to give them one last charge and challenge as to how they could keep living a life of victory after he passed on to his reward. Functioning as the instructor in verses 2–13, Joshua rehearsed sacred history up until that day, telling of all the mighty deeds of God on their behalf. Then verses 14–15 are some of the most famous in the Bible. Here Joshua serves as their chaplain, their spiritual leader. He gives a word of challenge and commitment we need to hear now, nearly 3,400 years later:

> "Therefore, fear the Lord and worship him in sincerity and truth. Get rid of the gods your ancestors worshiped beyond the Euphrates River and in Egypt, and worship the Lord. But if it doesn't please you to worship the Lord, choose for yourselves today: Which will you worship—the gods your ancestors worshiped beyond the Euphrates River or the gods of the Amorites in whose land you are living? As for me and my family, we will worship the Lord." (24:14–15 CSB)

After this call to commitment, look at the warning in verse 20 (CSB): "If you abandon the Lord and worship foreign gods, he will turn against you, harm you, and completely destroy you, after he has been good to you."

So Joshua is not only telling them how to possess their promised land but how to *preserve* their promised land. He's telling them not only how to claim their Canaan, but how to *keep* their Canaan. And in this passage, we find three commitments

Joshua calls them and us to make and keep. We find the first commitment in verse 14: "Fear the LORD."

1. Maintain Your Wonder

If we want to continue to walk in spiritual victory, we must maintain the wonder. We need to stand in reverence and respect, in awe and amazement before our great God. Reflect on his blessings in your life and thank him constantly. Don't become a casual Christian; never let the wonder wane.

In Exodus 20, God came down on the mountain with fire and smoke, lightning and thunder, blasts of a trumpet and shaking of the earth, and the people were terrified. And Moses said, "Don't be afraid." What were they afraid of? They were afraid of the God who is a consuming fire! They firmly believed that God could break out and destroy them in an instant! "Don't be afraid," Moses said, "God didn't bring you to this place to destroy you, but here is why God has revealed himself in this way—to test you in order that the fear of God will remain with you so you may not sin!" (Exod. 20:20, paraphrase).

We have a generation today that does not fear God. It is just as the Bible says in Romans 3:18: "There is no fear of God before their eyes." Consequently, every sin you can name in the world is also in the church—among those who claim to be God's people. We have lost a sense of the one true preservative against evil: the fear of God! Remove the fear of God, and people believe there is no boundary, no limit, no restraint, and they do as they please. But let's look at the truth of God's Word: "Be sure your sin will find you out" (Num. 32:33); "It is appointed for man to die once, and after that comes judgment" (Heb. 9:27); "For we must all appear before the judgment seat of Christ, so that each one may receive what is due for what he has done in the body, whether good or evil" (2 Cor. 5:10).

Our choices have consequences; there will be a day of reckoning. We need to recover a sense of proper respect and reverence, awe and amazement as we stand in the presence of his burning holiness. You may think, *Wait a minute, I thought we had a faith built on love, not fear.* Well, there's no contradiction between love and fear. The Bible says in 1 John that God is love and God is light—he is holy. And the correct response to God's love and God's holiness is love and fear. There's no contradiction there. The fear of the Lord is simply love on its knees. It has been well said: "He who fears God the most loves him the best."

Now there's a difference in the kind of fear we are to have based on our relationship with God. A slave fears his master's whip. But a son fears his Father's displeasure. And a true child of God fears God not just because he's afraid God is going to zap him when he gets out of line; he fears God because he *loves* God. So Joshua is challenging them and us to fear God and maintain the wonder. That's the first thing. Let's look at the second.

2. Maximize Your Worship

We see the second commitment in Joshua 24:14 (NIV): "Serve him with all faithfulness." Maintain the wonder and maximize your worship. The word "serve" here doesn't mean to run around doing something for the Lord. If that's all the Lord wanted, he could get the angels to do that for him, and they would do a better job than we ever could. Rather, the word means to pay homage, to bow down before the Lord, to worship our God. And notice how we are to worship him: "with all faithfulness."

Sincerity: The ESV translation says: "in sincerity." This Hebrew word was used of animals that were perfect and whole, without blemish. The word came to mean completely or wholeheartedly. So when Joshua says, "Worship the Lord in sincerity," he's saying, "Worship God with all that you have!"

Someone has said, "It doesn't take much of a man to be a Christian, it just takes all there is of him." Have you done that? Have you given Jesus Christ everything?

Truth is we are already his. First Corinthians 6:19–20 (NIV) says: "Do you not know that your bodies are temples of the Holy Spirit, who is in you, whom you have received from God? You are not your own, you were bought at a price. Therefore, honor God with your bodies." Have you simply said to God: "Lord, I worship you in sincerity, with all there is of me"? Are you encouraging that kind of worship among those in your charge? Let it be a sincere worship.

Scripturally: Second, let it be a scriptural worship. Joshua says: "serve him in sincerity and *in truth*." "In truth" is missing from some versions, but I assure you it is in the original and correctly rendered in the KJV. All the sincerity in the world is no good unless it is linked with truth. There are a lot of sincere people in this world who are sincerely wrong. Jesus said we are to worship God "in Spirit and in truth" (John 4:24). So if we want to preserve our possessions, keep our Canaan, and continue to conquer and walk in victory, we must worship the Lord whole-heartedly, in sincerity, and scripturally—in truth.

Steadfastly: Not only should it be a sincere and scriptural worship, it should be a steadfast worship (v. 15). We've got a lot of casual Christians today, who serve God when it fits their schedule, and they give when they've got extra. What we need is men to say, like Joshua did: "Hey, if everybody else wants to go on with this 'take it or leave it attitude,' fine, but as for me and for my house, we will serve the Lord! Lord, you can count on me. Lord, I will worship you in sincerity, scripturally, and stead-fastly." That's how we should maximize our worship.

3. Muster for Warfare

Joshua gives us a threefold call to commitment in these commands. The first command was to fear the Lord—maintain the wonder. The second command was to serve the Lord—maximize our worship. Now here's the third command (v. 14 NIV): "Throw away the gods your forefathers worshiped beyond the Euphrates River and in Egypt." This is a negative command. Let's put it this way: muster for warfare.

They had been out of Egypt for perhaps as long as eighty years. All the adults who had come out of Egypt died during forty years of wandering in the desert. Now in the promised land, very few Israelites remembered their former captivity, and yet Joshua is warning them: "You have come out of Egypt, and yet there is still some of Egypt in you. Put away those gods of Egypt."

You know it is hard to kill a weed, isn't it? Every spring throughout the summer and into the fall, gardeners and farmers wage war on weeds. Dandelions are difficult to get rid of; Bermuda grass is tough to stop. Just when you think you've got it all, it pops up again. And it is the same way with our sinful nature. The weeds of our old life can sprout again, and that sinful temptation we thought was defeated can rise up and bite you. The Bible says: "Let anyone who thinks that he stands take heed lest he fall" (1 Cor. 10:12). Joshua is talking about the danger of old idols making a comeback.

You might ask: "As a New Testament believer, do I have to worry about idols?" The answer is "Yes!" Truth is we have *many* idols today. An idol is anything or anyone you love more, fear more, serve more, or trust more than God. There may be things you conquered after you were saved and things you've put away, but they're gradually creeping back in. We wish we could tell you since we've been Christians for years, we don't have to fight any more. But we are still fighting the gods of Egypt. We still find those ugly weeds sprouting every now and then. Listen, the devil never gives up anything or anybody without some kind of a fight—and everybody is going to serve some kind of god. When you think that you are too mature in the faith and your walk with the Lord to drift backwards into the worship of idols, you are vulnerable to doing just that. Satan has not taken his eye off of you and will use your hubris to trap you.

Bottom Line: The ancient gods are still being worshiped today, even though now we may use different names. What about mammon, the god of money from Jesus's teaching? Materialism is one of the greatest forms of idolatry in America today. Our possessions possess us. We are slaves to things and making the money to buy them. What about the Greek god Bacchus, the god of inebriation and intoxication? People are still worshiping Bacchus by the millions. Alcoholism and drug addiction are destroying lives.

There's also the ancient goddess Ashtaroth, the goddess of fertility, and the more modern Greek goddess Aphrodite, the goddess of sex. This society is so sold out to those gods that people take their identity from their preferred sex act. They are known as LGBTQ: Lesbian, Gay, Bisexual, Transgender, and Queer. In fact, New York City lets you choose between thirty-one different sexual identities, which are protected. In fact, businesses that don't respect and accommodate an individual's chosen gender identity risk incurring six-figure fines under rules implemented by the city's Commission on Human Rights.[6] The list of protected gender identities is available online and includes options such as "gender queer, gender bender," "two spirit," "third sex," "androgynous," "gender gifted," and "pangender." They worship the goddess Aphrodite.

Not only has the Supreme Court decriminalized sodomy and legalized same-sex marriage, they are well on their way to criminalizing Christianity because we disagree with this sexual insanity on biblical grounds. Look at the preponderance of sex in media, advertising, and the pervasiveness of pornography on the web. There are all kinds of mobile apps to promote and enable this hook-up culture: Tinder, Blendr, Grindr, and there's OkCupid, Bumble, and Tingle, to name a few. This culture worships Aphrodite. And as a result, the Center for Disease Control reports there is an epidemic of STDs.[7] Many men who stop short of a hook-up are hung up on pornography to the point it has ruined their relationship with their wives. We still worship the old gods.

Then there is Hades, the god of death that is being worshiped today. And remember the god Molech? In the Old Testament, people put their newborns in the idol's arms, and their babies were burned alive as a sacrifice. We are still sacrificing children to Molech. Over 60 million abortions have happened in America since the Supreme Court said it was a woman's right to choose to sacrifice that child to the god of convenience. Then there is the Greek goddess Sophia, the goddess of wisdom—today called intellectualism. Kids are brainwashed by progressive professors and teachers to the point they cannot even function in the real world. They end up aimless, jobless, and essentially worthless as far as being productive citizens, living off their parents with their useless degrees in philosophy, climatology, creative writing, multicultural studies, Islamic studies, etc. Men, those old gods are still with us; we just give them new names.

Here is the challenge: Never lay down your sword, never coast, never kick back, fold your arms, and go to sleep when it comes to idolatry. Never think you're out of the battle, because you're not. You will battle with the world, the flesh, and the devil until the day you die. You will have to contend with idols until the Lord takes you home. So how are we to muster for warfare and put away these false gods?

Forcefully: First of all, put them away forcefully. I like what the NIV says here: "Throw them away." That doesn't mean stick them in the closet of your life and think because they're out of sight, they're out of mind, you've dealt with them, and it's done. Oh no. Tried that and it doesn't work. It takes a resolute and radical removal.

Fully: And second, do it fully, or you'll lose that conquered ground. Let's say you have surgery to remove a cancerous tumor, and the doctor says: "I took out 90 percent of that tumor." You wouldn't say: "Well, I only have a little cancer in me, I guess I'll live with it." You either get that cancer out or that cancer will get you.

Finally: Do it finally, once for all. Notice he says in verse 15: "Choose whom you will serve." The word "choose" means to take a hard look, to discriminate, to decide. It's tougher than ever to choose today, isn't it? Too many options. You go through the drive-through, and there are four panels of food, or eat at a restaurant, and there is a book of options presented to you. Or go to the grocery and there are eight different kinds of apples to choose from. People today have "decision anxiety"—it is too tough to choose.

Joshua forces the issue, doesn't he? Look at all the gods and decide which one you will serve, fear, trust, love, and worship. Do your comparative shopping and decide. But when you look at it, you'll find that there's no comparison. Exodus 15:11 says: "Who is like you, O LORD, among the gods." And God himself said in Isaiah 40:25 (NIV), "To whom will you compare me? Who is my equal?" God is saying: "Bring your biggest, baddest, and best gods, and I'll beat them all." All the Egyptian gods went down in flames, all the gods of the "-ites" in Canaan were defeated, so choose. Choose!

That was the challenge Elijah presented to King Ahab, Queen Jezebel, the 400 prophets of Baal, the 450 prophets of Asherah, and to all the Hebrew people: "How much longer will you waver, hobbling between two opinions? If the LORD is God, follow him! But if Baal, then follow him!" (1 Kings 18:21 NLT). What is he saying? CHOOSE! When the fire came down from heaven, the people chose: "The LORD, he is God!" (v. 39).

4. Mark the Way

Having laid out this call to commitment, Joshua doesn't just ask them to choose. He also provides the example. He sets the pace. He marks the way.

"As for me . . .": Having put his life on the line for these people on numerous occasions and leading them from victory to victory, Joshua takes his vast credibility like a massive pile of chips, as it were, and puts it all on the table. "As for me . . . ." Reminds us of Paul's audacious call to: "Follow my example, as I follow the example of Christ" (1 Cor. 11:1 NIV). The challenge of Joshua's example echoes down through the halls of history.

Indeed, Joshua's words, "As for me" can be found in the mouth of the most famous orator of the American Revolution in his most famous speech. On March 23, 1775, the Second Virginia Convention had convened at what is now St. John's Church in Richmond, away from the watchful eye of the Loyalist governor. They had assembled to consider some weighty matters concerning the British tyranny and oppression of the king of England. A thirty-nine-year-old delegate from Hanover County took a seat in the church with the others. He listened as many of his limp-wristed colleagues babbled on and on in favor of continued conciliatory measures and more pleading with Parliament. The longer he listened, the more his righteous indignation increased. Finally, this fiery country lawyer rose from his pew to address the wavering assembly of Virginians. With great passion in his voice, he presented a Joshua-like, "Choose this day" call to the men in that church:

> "Mr. President, it is natural to man to indulge in the illusions of hope . . . but . . . let us not deceive ourselves, sir. . . . If we wish to be free . . . we must fight! I repeat it, sir, we must fight! An appeal to arms and to the God of hosts [Psalm 59:5] is all that is left us! They tell us, sir, that we are weak; unable to cope with so formidable an adversary. But when shall we be stronger? Will it be the next week, or the next year? Will it be when we are totally disarmed, and when a British guard shall be stationed in every house? Shall we gather strength by irresolution and inaction . . . until our enemies shall have bound us hand and foot?
>
> Sir, we are not weak if we make a proper use of those means which the God of nature hath placed in our power. The millions of people, armed in the holy cause of liberty . . . are invincible by any force which our enemy can send against us. Besides, sir, we shall not fight our battles alone. There is a just God who presides over the destinies of nations, and who will raise up friends to fight our battles for us [2 Chron. 32:8]. The battle, sir, is not to the strong alone [Eccl. 9:11]; it is to the vigilant, the active, the brave. Besides, sir . . . there is no retreat but in submission and slavery! Our chains are forged! Their clanking may be heard on the plains of Boston! The war is inevitable—and let it come! I repeat it, sir, let it come.

It is in vain, sir, to extenuate the matter. Gentlemen may cry, 'Peace, Peace'—but there is no peace
[Jer. 6:14]. The war is actually begun! . . . Our breth-
ren are already in the field! Why stand we here idle
[Matt. 20:6]? What is it that gentlemen wish? What
would they have? Is life so dear, or peace so sweet, as
to be purchased at the price of chains and slavery?
Forbid it, Almighty God [Rom. 6:2]! I know not what
course others may take; but *as for me* [Josh. 24:15],
give me liberty or give me death!"[8]

There it is: "As for me"! When Patrick Henry finished laying
out the choice between slavery and liberty, in a speech literally
filled with biblical language, he concluded his argument just
like Joshua: "As for me"! We all know the rest of that story. At
that climactic moment, the call rang out in response: "To arms!"
And that speech helped fan the flames of revolution into a raging
inferno; and within less than a month, the first shots were fired
in the War of Independence.

Imagine Joshua, "God's General," summoning his strength,
his eyes flashing with fire, raising his voice with a shout: "As for
me"! He laid out the choice. He made clear the consequences.
He called for commitment. Now he is planting his flag. Like the
courageous reformer Martin Luther declared: "Here I stand, I
can do no other, so help me God"!

"And my house . . .": Then Joshua includes his family as the
spiritual leader: "As for me and my house." Although some rabbis
claimed that he married Rahab, the former prostitute from Jericho listed in the lineage of Jesus, there is no record in the Scriptures that Joshua married and had children.[9] Consequently, with
the absence of biblical proof, the best we can say is that by "my
house" Joshua meant the whole extended family of which he was

the patriarch. That's the sense in which Joshua declared he and his family would serve the Lord. It is important to recognize that when Joshua referred to his family, he was speaking of those alive at the time as well as future generations of his bloodline. As the patriarch and chaplain of his family he was establishing a legacy of obedience that he expected to be passed down through future generations.

When we put up a wall hanging that declares: "As for me and my house, we will serve the Lord" in our homes today, we are proclaiming very much the same thing Joshua did. The only difference is that a husband and father is probably thinking more of his immediate family, those who live "under his roof." Men, we have a solemn responsibility to make sure what goes on in the home honors God and is the kind of lifestyle laid out in his Word and modeled by Jesus.

Obviously, we can have more say on the external actions and activities than we can over the thoughts and intents of the heart. We can't dictate how our wife and kids feel, believe, and desire. The best we can do is communicate expectations, model them in a winsome and loving way, and pray for the Spirit of God to do only what he can do in their hearts. But don't for one minute think what we do doesn't matter. It does! In our Stand Courageous Conferences, Tony Perkins, President of Family Research Council, speaks on the role of chaplain and shares these startling statistics from a Swiss study conducted several years ago as reported in *Touchstone Magazine*:

> If both father and mother attend regularly, 33 percent of their children will end up as regular churchgoers, and 41 percent will end up attending irregularly. Only a quarter of their children will end up not practicing at all.

If the father is irregular and mother regular, only 3 percent of the children will subsequently become regulars themselves, while a further 59 percent will become irregulars. Thirty-eight percent will be lost.

If the father is non-practicing and mother regular, only 2 percent of children will become regular worshippers, and 37 percent will attend irregularly. Over 60 percent of their children will be lost completely to the church.

In short, if a father does not go to church, no matter how faithful his wife's devotions, only one child in 50 will become a regular worshiper. If a father does go regularly, regardless of the practice of the mother, between two-thirds and three-quarters of their children will become churchgoers (regular and irregular).[10]

Men, our spiritual leadership matters greatly. The numbers clearly demonstrate this fact. Consequently, "As for me and my house, we will serve the Lord" is a powerful promise to do the best we can to influence our children toward serving the God we serve. It is also a prayer that the children raised in our home and in the church will follow in our footsteps in the faith. Men, that is our role as chaplains. Lead by calling them to commitment while modeling it for them in a winsome way.

"We will serve the Lord": Joshua makes a very public commitment before God and all the people. There is nothing shy and reserved about Joshua. He takes a stand for the Lord that is out there for all to see. This is a good place to remind everyone our role as chaplains doesn't stop at the front door of our homes and with our families. Don't forget your chaplain role extends to your friends and coworkers.

My (Cureton's) dad told me just before he died that when he first came to follow the Lord seriously, he and a few others would meet for prayer before the workday started. Some of the guys at work used to mock and make fun of him and the others. They called my dad a "holy roller." But these men kept on praying together. In fact, Dad used to study his Bible during lunch break in his office, and when he went back to work, he left it on his desk. He marked with a red pen the "Roman Road to Salvation" in Paul's letter to the Romans:

- Romans 3:23: "For all have sinned and fall short of the glory of God."
- Romans 6:23: "For the wages of sin is death, but the gift of God is eternal life in Christ Jesus our Lord."
- Romans 5:8: "But God demonstrates his own love for us in this: while we were still sinners, Christ died for us."
- Romans 10:9–10: "That if you confess with your mouth, 'Jesus is Lord,' and believe in your heart that God raised Him from the dead, you will be saved. For it is with your heart that you believe and are justified, and it is with your mouth that you confess and are saved."
- Romans 10:13: "For everyone who calls on the name of the Lord will be saved."

My dad used to share the gospel with his coworkers using these verses. Then one day, he came in and his Bible was gone. Stolen. And he had almost forgotten about it when nearly a year later, one of the guys sheepishly poked his head in his office and said, "Hey Pete, I need to talk to you." The man had Dad's Bible in his hand and said, "I'm the one who took your Bible, and I wanted to bring this back to you, and tell you I'm sorry. I took it as a prank to begin with, but when I started reading some of those places you underlined, the Lord saved me!"

Men, you may never know the impact you have on other men simply by being a good example. Just by making your commitment public. Imagine what God could do through you if you became more intentional and vocal as a chaplain. Let's follow the example of Joshua, whose courageous call to commitment echoes through the ages!

BATTLE BUDDY GROUP GUIDE

Week 6 – Man as a Chaplain

▶ God Equips Us to Be Chaplains
LTG (RET.) Jerry Boykin from his book *Man to Man*

In February 1979, the government of Iran had been overthrown by a radical Shi'ite Imam—Ruhollah Khomeini—who would be known thereafter as Iran's Supreme Leader. His Islamic Revolution was a bloodbath. In the process, on November 4, 1979, a throng of Khomeini's fiery youthful followers invaded the U.S. Embassy, kidnapping fifty-three Americans and holding them hostage.

Delta's first assignment was to rescue them. I've written elsewhere about the challenges we faced and the disappointments we endured. But one unexpected incident remains in my memory.

We were in Egypt, preparing to deploy into the Iranian desert refueling area; from there our complex rescue plan would take us to Teheran and the American Embassy, after a few hours of hiding in the mountains outside of the city. Our staging base in Egypt was an old Russian MiG airfield. I was going through final checks on my gear when Charlie Beckwith walked up to me. "Jerry," he said, "I'm going to get all these men together tomorrow morning before we launch and I want you to say a prayer before we go."

I was astonished. Not since he and I talked about our mothers had Charlie expressed any interest at all in religion in general or my faith in particular, in fact most of the time I still wondered where I stood with him. Now he had startled me with a side of himself I never dreamed existed—Charlie conceded that he and his men would do well this time to enlist the help of a higher authority.

"Okay, Colonel," I told him. "I'll be ready."

Early the next morning, he gathered Delta in the hangar in a loose formation and climbed up on a makeshift wooden platform.

I stood off to Charlie's left. After he said some encouraging words to the men, he concluded, "We're ready for this mission. I have confidence in every one of you that you'll do your job and do it well."

Then he said, "I'm going to ask Jerry to come up here and say a prayer before we launch."

Before I could begin speaking, General James Vaught stepped forward. "I want to quote some Scripture," the general said. "In the book of Isaiah, the Bible says, 'And I heard the voice of the Lord saying, "Whom shall I send, and who will go for us?" And Isaiah said, "Here am I! Send me!"' Men, your country's counting on you. You've stepped forward and said, 'Here am I, send me.' God bless you!"

Vaught's words, which were from one of my favorite passages of the Bible, were a special blessing to me. And for the second time in less than an hour, I was surprised to find faith at work. I knew there were other men of faith in Delta, but no one really talked about it. We didn't have an active Bible study and we didn't have a chaplain. But now, faced with a mission in which obstacles and danger hovered over every phase, even the senior officers among us swept our culture of absolute self-reliance aside and acknowledged God.

I asked the men to bow their heads and pray with me. "Almighty God, we've placed ourselves in your hands. And we ask you to lead us and guide us so that we might liberate our fellow Americans. We ask for your hand of mercy to be upon us. We ask for wisdom and courage. We ask you to keep us safe, and to keep safe the people we're going after. Bring us all home to our families. And I pray this in Christ's name, Amen."

After a rousing rendition of "God Bless America," a loud shout went up. Each man walked back to his cot, grabbed his gear, crossed the tarmac and marched into the back of the C-141....

As I reflect on those hours and days of preparation, it's clear to me that whatever the circumstances, God had a way of getting the attention of His warriors, reminding us that He was holding our lives in His hands.

We can also see that He found a way to raise up "chaplains" when He needed them, thrusting some of us forward to provide spiritual guidance and encouragement when it was most important. On that memorable occasion, I was grateful that He chose to use me, but I felt totally inadequate at the time. It is just a reminder that God does not necessarily choose the equipped; He equips the chosen.[11] ◀

Group Debrief

When we think of the word "priest" or "chaplain," the image of an ordained minister or some other church-appointed leader or religious official probably comes to mind. As men, we are to be spiritual leaders, like a priest or chaplain, in our home or with the group God has given us. Many of us don't think of ourselves in this way. However, the apostle Peter wrote: "But you are a chosen race, a royal priesthood, a holy nation, a people for his possession, so that you may proclaim the praises of the one who called you out of darkness into his marvelous light" (1 Pet. 2:9 csb).

We are a priesthood called to proclaim his praises because of what he has done for us. In fact, Jesus tells his followers:

> "You are the light of the world. A city situated on a hill cannot be hidden. No one lights a lamp and puts it under a basket, but rather on a lampstand, and it gives light for all who are in the house. In the same way, let your light shine before others, so that they may see your good works and give glory to your Father in heaven." (Matt. 5:14–16 csb)

This means no matter where we are, no matter what our job title may be, each of us as believers is to represent Christ, who is the light of the world. We should live our lives in such a winsome way, just like General Boykin, so others will see God in us as we step up and be a chaplain, a priest, a spiritual leader.

Questions to Consider

- How can you live your life in such a way that reflects Matthew 5:16? How can you position yourself to serve as a chaplain?

- Obviously, the place to start your duties as chaplain is with your family or group. What are some practical things you can do as the chaplain? What are some key times you could serve as spiritual leader?

- Are there any hindrances to keep you from being looked to for spiritual leadership? What changes do you need to make?

- General Boykin observed: "God does not necessarily choose the equipped; He equips the chosen." Pray for his equipping to become the spiritual leader God has called you to be.

Conclusion

Commentators estimate that there were over 2 million people gathered to hear Joshua's final challenge. God's General had been with them in the wilderness for forty years and led them to cross the Jordan River and conquer Canaan. For over twenty years, the people had lived peacefully in the promised land. Now Joshua was 110 years old, ready to meet his Maker. Like a great chaplain and spiritual leader, he calls them to commitment, then leads the way by example. He's passing the torch to the next generation. He's telling them if they want to preserve their possessions and keep their Canaan, if they want to walk in spiritual victory, they need to do these five things:

1. "Fear the Lord"!
2. "Serve the Lord"!
3. "Throw away those idols"!
4. "Choose this day whom you will serve"! And finally, Joshua lays down a marker for all to hear, see, and follow:
5. "As for me and for my house, we will serve the LORD."

So, we want to encourage you:
- Maintain the wonder.
- Maximize your worship.

- Muster for warfare.
- Mark the way for everyone in your charge.

I (Boykin) may have retired from military service, but I will never retire from active service to Christ my Commander. When he calls me home, I want my sword to be red with the blood of the enemy of our souls. I want to go into the presence of my King muddy and bloody from battle. When I see Jesus, I will humbly bow before him, offering him my sword and my worship. Men, I hope you will join us as we stand courageous until we breathe our last and give our all. He is worthy!

Book Study
Discipleship Tool

Agenda

Getting Acquainted

You only get one chance to start. So having all the group members there to meet the other guys, learn names, and connect on a "level playing field" is crucial. DO NOT be so structured in following this conversation guide that you keep the Holy Spirit from moving in your group. This is intended to show you one way to navigate your time together.

Conversation Guide

The most important thing you're going to do as you start your group is LISTEN! The leader who is doing all the talking is not a great small group leader!

1. What happened last week that you are thankful for?
   ⊚ Everyone needs to answer briefly.
2. What challenge is happening in your life, family, or community?
   ⊚ Everyone needs to answer briefly.

3. Ask for a volunteer to pray for each person by name.
    ⊙ Pray for everyone by name.
    ⊙ Thank God for all the blessings on our lives.
    ⊙ Pray for the challenges we are facing.
4. Ask if everyone was able to read the assigned chapter.
5. Ask everyone to share one main takeaway from the chapter.
6. Work through the discussion questions in the back of the chapter.
7. Once everyone has had a chance to answer the questions at the end of the chapter, ask the following questions:
    ⊙ "From what you have read this week, and what we discussed today/tonight, what is your 'I will' statement? How are you going to apply this lesson/truth?"
    ⊙ Assign the next reading assignment/chapter for the group and confirm date and time of next meeting.
    ⊙ Ask, "Does anyone feel led to close in prayer?" If no one volunteers, then the group leader will voice a short prayer and close out the group.

Outline & Tips

Books

The first order of business is your BOOK ORDER! Be sure to order your books one month in advance from your first group meeting! It is critical that everyone leave your group on Launch Night with the book in hand.

When you realize that the average American reads 2.4 books per year, you begin to grasp the potential impact that reading one solid, Christian book can have on a person. And reading books in a high accountability context is more like graduate school than reading in a recliner. Knowing you're going to be held accountable for learning the key takeaways and have a conversation with your group about the book will make the learning experience really rich. The best group leaders share from their own "well" of knowledge and experience, so using a book that really spoke to you is best.

Calendar

One of the most "mission critical" activities you'll do at your first session will be setting the calendar for the season. You and your group will need to decide how often to meet as a group (weekly or bi-weekly) and how long you will meet. Set targets for when you will begin and end. This will prevent the meeting from taking too long (60–90 minutes is ideal).

Location & Group Size

Keep the groups small. (Five is the ideal number, but 4–6 is OK.) Divide larger groups into subgroups and have them work through the questions simultaneously. Plan in advance the location and environment for your group. Make sure you'll have a comfortable place for everyone. Whether around a dining room table, in a den, or in another location, be sure your location is conducive to conversation and prayer. All this will help draw quiet or shy people into the discussion.

Friend & Transparency

Another important thing is friendship! You're going to need to be a FRIEND to your group members! Invest in them by loving them unconditionally . . . this means loving them where they are, showing them that you're their friend, and listening to them intently. TRANSPARENCY is another important part of being a group leader! The books you will read together are important and the prayer time is critical, but the real impact of a mature group leader is in sharing his/her life experiences, both good and bad. This is invaluable.

Pray

Praying for your group and leading your group to pray for each other is huge. Be intentional about this orienting your group to God, encouraging your group to pray for each other and for you between sessions.

STAND COURAGEOUS
Pledge

I solemnly pledge before God to stand courageous as a man.

As the *Provider*, I pledge to work as God gives me strength and provide for the basic needs of my family. I will demonstrate my love by meeting their needs before my own. I will honor God by giving to his work and serving those in need. I will also provide direction, values, and a sense of identity for those in my charge.

As the *Instructor*, I pledge to teach our family about our own history. I will also instruct them about our godly heritage as Americans as the reason for patriotism and sacrifice. I will instill in the minds of my sons what it means to be masculine as God made us. I will train those in my care to honor authority, live responsibly, and fear God so as to leave a godly legacy.

As the *Defender*, I pledge to protect my loved ones, and if necessary, lay down my life for my wife and my family as Jesus Christ did for me. I will guard my home from destructive and sinful influences. I pledge to confront evil, pursue justice, and defend the weak and defenseless when attacked, including the unborn.

As the *Battle Buddy*, I pledge to develop a bond with another trustworthy, God-fearing man for prayer, encouragement, and accountability. I will also seek out a younger man who needs to be mentored and make a significant investment in his life. I promise to maintain communications with these men despite any bad decisions or distance, because I keep my commitments.

As the *Chaplain*, I pledge to seek God in prayer, obey his Word, do his will and be faithful to his church and encourage the same in my family. I will provide God's vision for my family and help them see what is happening through a biblical worldview. I will teach them to love God with all of their hearts, all of their minds, and all of their strength and will bless my children as the spiritual leader of my home. "As for me and my house, we will serve the LORD" (Josh. 24:15).

I pledge to stand courageous for God's glory for as long as I live. So help me God!

Signature _____

Date_____

STAND ON THE WORD
Bible Reading Plan

We encourage you to walk with God daily in his Word and lead those in your charge to do the same. Why? The Bible is literally "God-breathed" (2 Tim. 3:16). In other words, it is God's very word to us. The Bible answers the big questions like:

- *Why am I here?*
- *Where did I come from?*
- *Where am I going (life after death)?*
- *If God is good, why does evil and suffering exist?*

The Bible not only answers these big questions, it offers practical advice in areas such as:

- *How can I deal with feelings of fear or anger or guilt?*
- *How can I forgive when I cannot forget?*
- *What should I look for in a spouse?*
- *How can I have a successful marriage?*
- *How can I be a good parent?*
- *What is my spiritual gift and place in the church?*

We learned the verse in Bible school: "Your word is a lamp for my feet and a light on my path" (Ps. 119:105 csb). God's Word shows us the way forward in any area of life and on every question we face. So walk with God daily in his Word!

We offer a Bible Reading Plan to get started. It involves a commitment to read the Bible through chronologically over two years. In other words, each reading takes you through the Bible as events happen in history as far as it is possible. Reading God's Word will help you establish a fruitful walk with the God who made you and loves you. Whether you are single or married, this plan will enable you to lead your friends and family in daily reading of God's Word. The added benefit is you will all be reading the same text *together*. It will amaze you to see how God speaks sometimes in the same ways and at other times in different ways to each of you. Being on this journey together will build a spiritual synergy, a deep bond, and a sense of unity and purpose like nothing else you can do.

Visit FRC.org/Bible to access it or simply text the word "Bible" to the number 67742. We can send reminders by email or text when you sign up. There are also daily questions you can forward to family members as a way of helping them engage the biblical text. Plus, there is a discussion guide to accompany the readings so you can debrief with your family, friends, small group, etc. once a week. This plan will enable you to fulfill your biblical role as the spiritual leader, the chaplain of your home or group of friends. Use it to impart the word of life.

About the Authors

LTG (RET.) JERRY BOYKIN
Executive Vice President, FRC

LTG (RET.) Jerry Boykin serves as Family Research Council's Executive Vice President. He was one of the original members of the U.S. Army's Delta Force. He was privileged to ultimately command these elite warriors in combat operations. Later, he commanded all the Army's Green Berets as well as the Special Warfare Center and School. In all, General Boykin spent over thirty-six years in the army, serving his last four years as the Deputy Undersecretary of Defense for Intelligence. He is an ordained minister with a passion for spreading the gospel of Jesus Christ and encouraging Christians to become warriors in God's Kingdom. He and his wife, Ashley, enjoy spending time with their five children and growing number of grandchildren. He is the author of *Man to Man*, *Never Surrender*, and coauthor of several books, including *The Warrior's Soul* with Dr. Stu Weber.

DR. KENYN M. CURETON
Vice President for Christian Resources, FRC

Dr. Kenyn Cureton serves as the Vice President for Christian Resources with a mission of equipping Christians to become spiritually active, governance-engaged conservatives (i.e., SAGECONS). Previously he served as VP for Church Ministries for over twelve years. Serving to implement the vision of FRC President Tony Perkins, the "Watchmen on the Wall" pastors network grew from 1,800 to over 40,000 who were engaged by email, and the number of Culture Impact Teams in all 50 states grew to over 9,000. Prior to joining FRC, Dr. Cureton served as Vice President for Convention Relations for the Southern Baptist Convention (SBC) after serving as a pastor for twenty years. Dr. Cureton is the author of the *Voter Impact Toolkit*, the *Culture Impact Team Manual*, a daily devotional titled *Lost Episodes: Daily Inspiration from America's Amazing Story*, as well as other church resources. Kenyn and his wife, Pat, have two adult married children and enjoy spoiling their grandchildren.

Notes

Introduction

1. https://www.navy.mil/MEDAL-OF-HONOR-RECIPIENT-EDWARD-C-BYERS-JR/#cit.

2. See Dilip Joseph and James Lund, *Kidnapped by the Taliban: A Story of Terror, Hope, and Rescue by SEAL Team Six* (Nashville: Thomas Nelson, 2014).

3. Official Citation for Edward C. Byers Jr., United States Navy, February 29, 2016, https://www.navy.mil/MEDAL-OF-HONOR-RECIPIENT-EDWARD-C-BYERS-JR/#cit.

4. http://catholicphilly.com/2016/03/news/national-news/catholic-navy-seal-given-medal-of-honor-for-heroic-action-in-afghanistan/. See also http://www.kofc.org/en/news-room/articles/weight-of-valor.html.

Chapter 1

1. Tucker Carlson, "Men in America," Four-Part Series, Fox News Channel, March 2018, https://www.youtube.com/watch?v=LrhHkQhglig&t=341s.

2. Daniel Davis, "What's Driving America's 'Boy Crisis,'" *Daily Signal*, August 1, 2019, https://www.dailysignal.com/2019/08/01/whats-driving-americas-boy-crisis/. They quote Dr. Warren Farrell, coauthor of *The Boy Crisis: Why Our Boys Are Struggling and What We Can Do About It* (Dallas: BenBella Books, 2018). See also: Mark Meckler, "Of 27 Deadliest Mass Shooters, 26 of Them Were Fatherless," RealClear Politics, February 27, 2018, https://www.realclearpolitics.com/2018/02/27/of_27_deadliest_mass_shooters_26_of_them_were_fatherless_435596.html#!

3. Barna Group in partnership with Josh McDowell Ministries, *The Porn Phenomenon: The Impact of Pornography in a Digital Age* (2016), 142.

4. Tucker Carlson, Men in America, Four Part Series, FOX News Channel, March 2018. See https://www.youtube.com/watch?v=LrhHkQ

hglig for part 1 on March 7, 2018. See https://www.youtube.com/
watch?v=FJVN_ReJD00 for part 2 on March 14, 2018. See https://www.
youtube.com/watch?v=QgHzvUyb-Bw for part 3 on March 21, 2018. See
https://www.youtube.com/watch?v=n0wCBFNTVhk&t=175s for part 4 on
March 28, 2018.

5. Maya Salam, "What Is Toxic Masculinity?" *New York Times*, January
22, 2019, https://www.nytimes.com/2019/01/22/us/toxic-masculinity.html.

6. "We Believe: The Best Men Can Be | Gillette (Short Film)," Gillette,
January 13, 2019, https://www.youtube.com/watch?v=koPmuEyP3a0.

7. "APA Guidelines for Psychological Practice with Boys and Men,"
American Psychological Association, 2018, https://www.apa.org/about/
policy/boys-men-practice-guidelines.pdf.

8. "Brown University Offering Programs for 'Unlearning Toxic
Masculinity,'" Fox News Insider, October 25, 2018, https://insider.foxnews.
com/2018/10/25/brown-university-offering-programs-unlearning-toxic-
masculinity-greg-gutfeld-reacts.

9. Glenn Harlan Reynolds, "Higher education discriminates against
men, but Title IX complaints may change that," *USA Today*, February
12, 2019, https://www.usatoday.com/story/opinion/2019/02/12/colleges-
universities-discriminate-men-title-ix-complaints-toxic-masculinity-
column/2831834002/.

10. Robert Kraychik, "Woke West Point Curriculum Denounces
'Toxic Masculinity,'" *Breitbart*, January 28, 2020, https://www.breitbart.
com/tech/2020/01/28/woke-west-point-curriculum-denounces-toxic
-masculinity/.

11. Matthew Henry, *Matthew Henry's Concise Commentary on the Bible*,
Genesis 2:4.

12. Unless otherwise noted, statistics in this section are found in
"Towards a Conceptual Model of How Society Works: The Tasks of Living,
the Basic Institutions and the Dynamics of Belonging or Rejection,"
presented by Patrick F. Fagan, Ph.D., Senior Fellow, Family Research Council
at the Annual Conference of the Society of Catholic Social Scientists St John's
University School of Law, October 27, 2007.

13. Linda Waite and Maggie Gallagher, *The Case for Marriage: Why
Married People Are Happier, Healthier and Better Off Financially* (New York:
Doubleday, 2000), 85.

14. Polly House, "Want your church to grow? Then bring in the men,"
Baptist Press, April 3, 2003, http://www.bpnews.net/15630/want-your-
church-to-grow-then-bring-in-the-men. Statistics from *Promise Keeper at
Work* (Focus on the Family Publishing, 1996).

15. LTG (RET.) William G. Boykin, *Man to Man: Rediscovering
Masculinity in a Challenging World* (Nashville: Fidelis Books, 2020), 19–21.

Chapter 2: Man as a Provider

1. As quoted in John Mack Faragher, *Daniel Boone: The Life and Legend of an American Pioneer* (New York: Henry Holt and Company, 1993), 65.

2. Joseph Banvard, *The American Statesman: or, Illustrations of the Life and Character of Daniel Webster Designed for American Youth* (Boston: D. Lothrop & Co., 1875), 30–31.

3. Henry T. Blackaby, Richard Blackaby, and Claude King, *Experiencing God: Knowing and Doing the Will of God*, Revised and Expanded (Nashville: B&H Publishing Group, 2008), 61.

4. Claire Z. Cardona and Tom Steele, "Dog-rescue pilot who went off-course over Texas and never landed may have lost oxygen," *Dallas Morning News*, January 7, 2018, https://www.dallasnews.com/news/2018/01/07/dog -rescue-pilot-who-went-off-course-over-texas-and-never-landed-may -have-lost-oxygen/.

5. LTG (RET.) William G. Boykin, *Man to Man: Rediscovering Masculinity in a Challenging World* (Nashville: Fidelis Books, 2020), 17–18.

Chapter 3: Man as an Instructor

1. Credit for the outline goes to Dr. Adrian Rogers and his sermon on this passage. Visit lwf.org.

2. Erik Sherman, "America Is the Richest, and Most Unequal, Country," *Fortune*, September 30, 2015, http://fortune.com/2015/09/30/ america-wealth-inequality/.

3. Megan Brenan, "American Pride Hits New Low; Few Proud of Political System," Gallup, July 2, 2019, https://news.gallup.com/poll/259841/ american-pride-hits-new-low-few-proud-political-system.aspx.

4. Charles Dean, ed., *Discourse Concerning Western Planting: Written in the Year 1584 by Richard Hakluyt, Now First Printed from a Contemporary Manuscript with a Preface and an Introduction by Leonard Woods* (Cambridge: John Wilson and Son, 1877), 158.

5. "The First Charter of Virginia; April 10, 1606," Yale Law School, http://avalon.law.yale.edu/17th_century/va01.asp.

6. "Baptism of Pocahontas," Encyclopedia Virginia, https://www .encyclopediavirginia.org/media_player?mets_filename=evm00002822 mets.xml.

7. "The First Legislative Assembly," National Park Service, https://www. nps.gov/jame/learn/historyculture/the-first-legislative-assembly.htm.

8. "Agreement Between the Settlers at New Plymouth: 1620," Yale Law School, http://avalon.law.yale.edu/17th_century/mayflower.asp.

9. William Bradford, *Of Plymouth Plantation 1620–1647*, ed. Samuel Morrison (New York: Alfred A. Knopf, 2001), 95.

10. Ibid., 120–21.

11. Governor John Winthrop, "A Model of Christian Charity," The Winthrop Society, https://www.winthropsociety.com/doc_charity.php.

12. "The Articles of Confederation of the United Colonies of New England; May 19, 1643," Yale Law School, https://avalon.law.yale.edu/17th_century/art1613.asp.

13. "Fundamental Orders of 1639," Yale Law School, http://avalon.law.yale.edu/17th_century/order.asp.

14. See Max Weber, *The Protestant Ethic and the Spirit of Capitalism*, trans. by Talcott Parsons (New York: Charles Scribner's and Sons, 1958).

15. See "Religion and the Founding of the American Republic," Library of Congress, https://www.loc.gov/exhibits/religion/rel04.html.

16. "Congressional Prayer Room," Office of the Chaplain – U.S. House of Representatives, http://chaplain.house.gov/religion/prayer_room.html.

17. Worthington Chauncey Ford, ed., *The Writings of George Washington* (New York and London: G. P. Putnam's Sons, 1890), 10:845. See https://oll.libertyfund.org/titles/2414#Washington_1450-10_845.

18. "Transcript of Treaty of Paris (1783)," OurDocuments.gov, https://www.ourdocuments.gov/doc.php?flash=false&doc=6&page=transcript.

19. James Madison, *Notes of Debates in the Federal Convention of 1787* (Athens, Ohio: Ohio University Press, 1985), 209–10.

20. "Complete version of 'The Star-Spangled Banner' showing spelling and punctuation from Francis Scott Key's manuscript in the Maryland Historical Society collection," National Museum of American History, https://amhistory.si.edu/starspangledbanner/pdf/ssb_lyrics.pdf.

21. "Second Inaugural Address," Abraham Lincoln Online, http://www.abrahamlincolnonline.org/lincoln/speeches/inaug2.htm.

22. "Legacy," Sergeant York Patriotic Foundation, http://sgtyork.org/christian.

23. "A 'Mighty Endeavor:' D-Day," Franklin D. Roosevelt Presidential Library and Museum, https://www.fdrlibrary.org/d-day.

24. "Transcript of General Dwight D. Eisenhower's Order of the Day (1944)," OurDocuments.gov, https://www.ourdocuments.gov/doc.php?flash=false&doc=75&page=transcript.

25. LTG (RET.) William G. Boykin, *Man to Man: Rediscovering Masculinity in a Challenging World* (Nashville: Fidelis Books, 2020), 43–44.

Chapter 4: Man as a Defender

1. "Morristown Shooting," Tennessee Gun Owners, May 9, 2010, https://www.tngunowners.com/forums/topic/25457-morristown-shooting/.

2. John Piper, *This Momentary Marriage: A Parable of Permanence* (Wheaton, IL: Crossway, 2009), 91.

3. Bird Wilson., ed., *The Works of the Honourable James Wilson, L.L.D., Late One of the Associate Justices of the Supreme Court of the United States, and Professor of Law in the College of Philadelphia,* 3 vols. (Philadelphia: Bronson and Chauncey, 1804), 3:83–85. Bracketed items added.

4. Joe Carter, "A brief introduction to the just war tradition: Jus ad bellum," Ethics & Religious Liberty Commission, August 17, 2017, https://erlc.com/resource-library/articles/a-brief-introduction-to-the-just-war-tradition-jus-ad-bellum.

5. Jared Sparks, ed., *The Writings of George Washington; being his Correspondence, Addresses, Messages, and other Papers, Official and Private, Selected and Published from the Original Manuscripts with a Life of the Author, Notes and Illustrations,* 12 vols. (Boston: Ferdinand Andrews, 1834–38), 12:8, from his First Annual Address to Congress on January 8, 1790.

6. Richard Henry Lee, *An Additional Number of Letters from the Federal Farmer to the Republican* (New York: 1788), 170, Letter XVIII, January 25, 1788.

7. Guy Gugliotta, "New Estimate Raises Civil War Death Toll," *New York Times*, April 2, 2012, https://www.nytimes.com/2012/04/03/science/civil-war-toll-up-by-20-percent-in-new-estimate.html.

8. The Barna Report in partnership with Josh McDowell Ministries, *The Porn Phenomenon: The Impact of Pornography in the Digital Age* (Barna Group, 2016), 142.

9. Ibid.

10. "10 Ways to Fight Pornography," Josh McDowell Ministry, https://www.josh.org/10-ways-fight-pornography/.

11. "The Consequences of Roe v. Wade?" National Right to Life, January 2019, https://www.nrlc.org/uploads/NRLNews/NRLNewsJan2019.pdf.

12. https://www.thegospelcoalition.org/article/clarity-not-gadgetry-pro-life-apologetics-for-the-next-generation/

13. "Know the Facts," A21, A21.org/facts.

14. LTG (RET.) William G. Boykin, *Man to Man: Rediscovering Masculinity in a Challenging World* (Nashville: Fidelis Books, 2020), 65–68.

Chapter 5: Man as a Battle Buddy

1. Stand Courageous Conference Call on March 30, 2021. Visit https://standcourageous.com/listen.

2. https://standcourageous.com/podcast

3. Edited from Stu Weber, Battle Buddy Presentation, Stand Courageous Conference, Woodland Park, Colorado, June 19, 2021.

4. LTG (RET.) William G. Boykin, *Man to Man: Rediscovering Masculinity in a Challenging World* (Nashville: Fidelis Books, 2020), 103–5.

Chapter 6: Man as a Chaplain

1. Tony Perkins, transcript from Stand Courageous Conference in Woodland Park, Colorado, June 19, 2021.

2. Noah Brooks, "Personal Recollections of Abraham Lincoln," *Harper's Weekly*, July 1865, 222–30. See https://harpers.org/archive/1865/07/personal-recollections-of-abraham-lincoln/.

3. William J. Johnson, *George Washington the Christian* (Arlington Heights, IL: Christian Liberty Press, 1991/1992), 197–98.

4. Jared Sparks, ed., *The Writings of George Washington,* 12 vols. (Boston: American Stationer's Company, 1837), 12:399–411 for this and other evidences presented regarding his faith.

5. Dr. Ligon Duncan, "The Family Altar," sermon on Deuteronomy 6:4–6 delivered on June 30, 2002. See https://rts.edu/resources/the-family-alter/ accessed on September 28, 2021.

6. Peter Hasson, "New York City Lets You Choose from 31 Different Gender Identities," *Daily Caller*, May 24, 2016, http://dailycaller.com/2016/05/24/new-york-city-lets-you-choose-from-31-different-gender-identities/#ixzz4PtIQyJ4r.

7. "Reported Cases of Sexually Transmitted Diseases on the Rise, Some at Alarming Rate," CDC, November 17, 2015, http://www.cdc.gov/nchhstp/newsroom/2015/std-surveillance-report-press-release.html.

8. William Wirt, *Sketches of the Life and Character of Patrick Henry* (Philadelphia: James Webster, 1817), 120–23. Bracketed items added.

9. See the Babylonian Talmud, *Megillah 14T*:

> Rav Nahman responded to Eina the Elder and said to him . . . For Rahab converted and married Joshua, and therefore Huldah (the prophetess) descended from both Joshua and Rahab. The Gemara raises a difficulty: But did Joshua have any descendants? But isn't it written in the genealogical list of the tribe of Ephraim: "Nun his son, Joshua his son" (I Chronicles 7:27)? The listing does not continue any further, implying that Joshua had no sons. The Gemara answers: Indeed, he did not have sons, but he did have daughters.

See https://jwa.org/encyclopedia/article/rahab-midrash-and-aggadah, accessed September 30, 2021.

10. The study is from Werner Haug and Phillipe Warner, "The Demographic Characteristics of the Linguistic and Religious Groups in Switzerland" in Werner Haug, et al. eds., *The Demographic Characteristics of National Minorities in Certain European States* (Strasbourg: Council of Europe Directorate General III, Social Cohesion, 2000) as cited by Robbie Low, "The Truth about Men & Church," in *Touchstone Magazine* (June

2003). See https://www.touchstonemag.com/archives/article.php?id=16-05-024-v, accessed on September 30, 2021.

11. LTG (RET.) William G. Boykin, *Man to Man: Rediscovering Masculinity in a Challenging World* (Nashville: Fidelis Books, 2020), 114–16.

BE ALERT, **STAND** FIRM IN THE FAITH,
BE **COURAGEOUS**, BE STRONG.
1 Corinthians 16:13

STAND COURAGEOUS

MEN'S MINISTRY & CONFERENCES

*Where men can discover a model of biblical manhood,
leadership, and strength—equipping and challenging
men to be all God has designed them to be.*

To inquire about our ministry or hosting a conference,
email StandCourageous@frc.org

SUBSCRIBE
to our email list

**JOIN OUR
TEXT LIST**
by texting
MEN to 67742

DOWNLOAD
the
SC APP

Get the App